(E)Merging Identities:
Graduate Students in the Writing Center

by

Melissa Nicolas, editor

Fountainhead Press X Series for Professional Development

Series edited by
Allison D. Smith and Trixie G. Smith

Cover design by Pat Bracken

Page design by Cathy Spitzenberger

Copyright © 2008   Fountainhead Press

Books may be purchased for educational purposes.

For information, please call or write:

　　　1-800-586-0330

　　　Fountainhead Press
　　　100 W. Southlake Blvd., Suite 142, #350
　　　Southlake, TX 76092

Web site: www.fountainheadpress.com
E-mail: customerservice@fountainheadpress.com

First Edition
ISBN 978-1-59871-184-4

Printed in the United States of America

Acknowledgements

As most writing center projects do, this one started over food (and belly dancing!). At International Writing Centers Association in Savannah, Georgia, a small group of us interested in the issues brought to light in this collection first gathered to share our experiences. At some point after the dinner and before the belly dancing, someone suggested that there should be a book about graduate students in the writing center. This collection grew out of that comment.

I would especially like to acknowledge Beth Rapp Young, an attendee of that dinner and an early collaborator on this project. Beth played an instrumental role in designing the call for papers, making initial editing decisions, and shaping the preliminary direction of this collection. While Beth's input was invaluable, any errors or mistakes in the following pages are mine.

Finally, I wish to acknowledge the importance of my time as a graduate student in the writing center as an administrator, tutor, and client. My years in the writing center in these different roles shaped my future scholarship, teaching, and administration in ways that I am just now beginning to understand.

Table of Contents

PART 1

BETWIXT:
The Complexities of Graduate Student Life in the Writing Center

PART II

BETWEEN:
The Ways Graduate Students
Challenge Writing Center Theory and Practice

Foreword

While you're in the midst of it, graduate school seems like it will never end, but it's really a very transitory space designed for intense study and practice—practice teaching, tutoring, and, for some, administering, as well as learning to balance, negotiate, and emerge. At least Allison and I had graduate experiences like this.

As an undergraduate, I worked as a peer tutor, actually the first peer tutor at my small college's brand new center. I was chosen because I was a double major in English and Education; I had no idea that there were people in academe actually theorizing about writing centers and tutoring. It would be ten more years and two writing centers later before I discovered the National Writing Center Association and its regionals or publications like the *Writing Lab Newsletter* and the *Writing Center Journal.* It was this third center, at the University of South Carolina (USC), where I discovered writing center theory and its intersections with comp/rhet and Writing Across the Curriculum/Writing In the Disciplines (WAC/WID). Here I also discovered the possibilities of focusing my research on writing centers, of creating a career in writing centers, and of gaining the experience needed for such a profession by working as a Graduate Student Administrator (GSA). In fact, USC provided the opportunity to work as a GSA in the main center run by the English Department and then in the Center for Business Communication (CBC) located in the Darla Moore School of Business. These centers provided space for my *(E)Merging Identities* within the broad field of composition and rhetoric. Allison had similar experiences as tutor, teacher, and administrator in writing labs, first-year composition programs, and English as a Second Language (ESL) programs at California State Long Beach and the University of Illinois.

As many of the essays in this collection explain, at times it is tough to be a peer and an administrator. At South Carolina my colleagues and I found ways to negotiate these difficulties by drawing on what our director, Jean Bohner, called the Complementary Expertise model. We each had something to offer and had to find ways to listen to each other and to our students, so we could provide the best writing help possible. Of course, we each had to figure out how to define and subsequently manage our own varied roles as we worked in the center, taught classes, took classes, and eventually completed our programs. At that time, no guidelines existed for GSAs; we were all figuring it out in our individual locations—which is why the history of the International Writing Centers Association (IWCA) Position Statement on GSAs presented in this collection is so important.

Other essays in this collection attest to the importance of mentoring, negotiating power, and figuring out what it means to be a graduate student/tutor, as opposed to an undergraduate tutor—how does it affect training or education, how does it affect the language of sessions, how does it affect the relationships between tutors, GSAs, directors, faculty, teaching assistants (TAs), administrators, and others? Allison and I both remember turning to directors and other administrators as mentors; Martha Thomas, my director in the CBC, was very good at negotiating the differences in thinking and pedagogy that existed in the CBC, and she was also talented at framing her memos, letters, budgets, and other paperwork for the various audiences we encountered, but most importantly, she was willing to share her secrets.

The lessons learned as a graduate student were invaluable to our growth as scholars, teachers, and administrators—our professional development. They are why Allison and I started our own GSA program at Middle Tennessee State, for both the writing center and the TAs. It is also why I maintain a mentoring program in my present center. These lessons are also why we are excited about this collection of essays for the *Fountainhead Press X Series for Professional Development*. The reflections, reports, and arguments presented here should be illuminating for directors who have graduate tutors in their centers, graduate students who are working in centers or considering how to make the center a part of their career path, and undergraduate tutors who question what's next, as well as program advisors, dissertation directors, and anyone else who wonders about the struggles and triumphs of graduate students in the writing center.

Trixie G. Smith

Fall 2007

Introduction
(E)Merging Identities: Authority, Identity, and the Place(s) In-Between

Melissa Nicolas

In-between spaces are murky, stressful, overwhelming, exasperating, challenging, exciting, hopeful, and full of potential. Inhabiting an in-between place, whether professionally or personally, puts our minds in over-drive. We ask questions; we do research; we seek advice from loved ones, friends, and counselors; we play out scenarios about possible ways to move from in-between to actually arriving at a decision, a destination, a resolution. During this in-between time, we often experience moments of great clarity about who we are and what we want, quickly followed by moments of intense self-doubt and questions about our identity. Being in-between causes us to assess our situation and reflect on our strengths and weaknesses in order to accept or reject roles and to negotiate this liminal space.

In terms of academic culture, there is no greater in-between space than that of being a graduate student, especially being a graduate student in an English program since many graduate students hold teaching, tutoring, and/or administrative appointments. On the one hand, graduate students are most definitely *students*, people who are learning about and becoming initiated into a field or discipline. On the other hand, these same students are often given institutional roles, like teaching their own classes, or tutoring, or running a writing program, that give them a greater level of institutional authority and responsibility than undergraduate students and even some of their graduate peers. Graduate students, in many ways, are betwixt and between: they are not faculty, yet they may share some of the same duties as faculty; they are not fully credentialed in their field, yet they may be called on to use their knowledge to run, or at least assist with running, a writing program or writing center. Composition scholars have begun to address the complexity of graduate students' place in English programs, particularly with regard to Writing Program Administration (WPA) work (see Anson and Rutz; Fontaine; Miller et al; *Rhetoric Review* 21.1; Powell, et al.), and the writing center community has begun exploring the complex roles our graduate students play in shaping both theory and practice. It is not uncommon today, for example, for graduate programs in composition and rhetoric to offer a course on either writing center administration, in particular, or writing center administration in the larger context of WPA work (Jackson, Leverenz, and Law).

Even though writing center work has become increasingly professionalized (Jackson, Leverenz, and Law), the role of graduate students in writing center work remains ambiguous. This ambiguity may be largely a result of the very purpose of writing centers to occupy a sort of academic middle ground (Harris). In the writing center environment, therefore, traditional academic roles become blurred because writing centers' existence outside of the traditional classroom yet still within the institution mark them as liminal spaces. According to Bonnie Sunstein, this liminality allows for those who inhabit the center to experiment with different roles: "teachers who are tutors, writers who are readers, people who speak their written texts" (7) interact with each other in multiple ways. In the case of graduate students in the writing center, then, we have students who are, by virtue of their positions as graduate students, already in an in-between place, taking on various roles in an environment that is also liminal. Regardless of the role(s) graduate students play in the center—client, tutor, or administrator—their situation is one of constant negotiation.

Graduate student clients must negotiate their position vis-à-vis their tutor who may be a fellow graduate student with more (or less) schooling than the client but who could just as likely be an undergraduate tutor or, on occasion, even a faculty tutor. In addition, Nancy Welch explains that graduate students often come to the writing center struggling with what they see as a "strict choice between resistance or assimilation" to dominant academic discourse (5). Welch believes that the writing center, as a liminal site, is uniquely positioned to assist graduate students with this struggle, not necessarily by pointing the writer in one direction or another, but by offering an opportunity for graduate student writers to explore the multiple directions open to them. In this way, the writing center becomes not, "an either/or crossroads but a busy, noisy, fascinating intersection, opening out into many more than just two roads that might be taken" (19). By being a noisy intersection, writing centers are a site where graduate student clients can test out ideas, hypothesize, and experiment without fear of judgment or evaluation. At the same time, though, "when graduate students come to the writing center, everyone's expertise is at stake: the graduate student's expertise in a particular discipline, the tutor's expertise in writing and tutoring, and the disciplinary professor's expertise as a teacher-mentor" (Leverenz 50–51).

Like graduate student clients, graduate student tutors are also at a busy intersection when it comes to negotiating their role and authority in the writing center. This negotiation is especially complex for graduate student tutors because so much writing center literature emphasizes non-hierarchical, peer relationships as the foundation of client-tutor interaction (see Harris; Lunsford), but the majority of writing center clients are undergraduates. As Connie Snyder Mick observes, the relationship between the authority of a graduate student tutor, an undergraduate client, and the supposed "peer" relationship that undergirds so much writing center practice is bound to cause "cognitive dissonance" for graduate tutors as well as their undergraduate clients (37–40).

Cognitive dissonance is also a consideration if graduate students have some administrative responsibilities in the center (indeed, sometimes a graduate student is the director for the center) because they will have much of the responsibility of a faculty member but none of the status while, at the same time, they may hold slightly more authority than some of the other graduate students in the center whom the graduate administrator may be supervising. Graduate student administrators must navigate through complex institutional waters as they engage in the day-to-day tasks of running a writing center—tasks that are often more frequently the province of faculty such as requesting funding or handling complaints about the writing center from faculty or other administrators. As Catherine Latterell explains, graduate student WPAs inhabit a "liminal, interstitial space somewhere between faculty status and student status" (35). The liminal state of graduate student WPAs creates a complex set of political, educational, and institutional circumstances (also see Eckerle, Rowan, and Watson) that call on WPAs to constantly consider their position(s) in the academic hierarchy.

While graduate students play such prominent, complex, and vital roles in the writing center, discussion of these issues has been limited to occasional journal articles or single chapters in edited collections (see Conroy, Lerner and Siska; Leverenz). The purpose of *(E)Merging Identities: Graduate Students in the Writing Center,* then, is to provide a forum for focusing on issues that are most germane to graduate students' experiences in the writing center. Authors in this collection address such questions as: How do graduate students navigate through the complicated work of being tutors and teachers, often simultaneously? What is the nature of the relationship between a graduate tutor and graduate client? an undergraduate client? What can/should the writing center do for graduate student clients? What is/should be the relationship between a faculty director and a graduate student administrator? How do graduate students as administrators negotiate peer relationships with other graduate students in the center, especially those with whom they might have authority over by virtue of being an administrator? What are the benefits and drawbacks of working in and doing research on writing centers as a graduate student?

Until quite recently, there seemed to be an underlying assumption in much writing center literature that all tutors, clients, and administrators (regardless of institutional rank) share similar concerns and occupy similar roles. However, as the essays in this collection illustrate, graduate students in the writing center are constantly aware of the multiple power dynamics that are at play in the center, and the presence of graduate students in our centers should challenge us to re-think some of our foundational assumptions about the concerns and roles of writing center clients, tutors, and administrators.

Considering that graduate students—inhabiting a middle place between student and scholar—can and often do occupy the roles of client, tutor, and administrator, conceivably even within the same day, the writing center as an in-between place is a particularly fruitful site for exploring the ways in which graduate students negotiate this merging of identities while their own identities as authors, tutors, scholars, and administrators are emerging.

Organization

Part I: Betwixt: The Complexities of Graduate Student Life in the Writing Center

As much writing center literature does, this collection begins with some personal narratives in order to demonstrate how the issues that surface throughout the collection affect the lived experience of graduate students in the writing center.

First, Michael Mattison, in a letter to his younger self, creatively explores the ways he surprisingly found himself engaged in writing center work, first as a tutor and then as an administrator. Throughout, Mattison provides examples of the real struggles he faced as he negotiated his authority as student, teacher, and administrator. In chapter two, Nathalie Singh-Corcoran continues the narrative thread by sharing the unfavorable reactions she received from faculty—even faculty in writing center studies—about her desire to pursue writing center scholarship.

Mattison and Singh-Corcoran's essays do much to articulate the complexities of writing center work for graduate students, and in chapter three, Julie Eckerle, Karen Rowan, and Shevaun Watson explain how their engagement with this complexity led them to draft the IWCA "Statement on Graduate Student Writing Center Administration." As they explain in this chapter, these co-authors wish to see this position statement become a "living document," one that will provide a point of reference for both graduate students and faculty as they work together to assure that graduate students as writing center administrators receive the professional support and development opportunities that they need in order to become full participants in the writing center community in particular and the academy at large.

One of the main tenets of the position statement is that graduate student administrators should have the guidance of a faculty or professional director to support their work as fledgling administrators. Chapters four and five provide examples of what these mentoring relationships might look like. In chapter four, Leigh Ryan and Lisa Zimmerelli describe the mentoring relationship they have negotiated as they have worked together first as faculty (Ryan) and graduate student (Zimmerelli) and then as peers. In the following chapter, Katherine Tirabassi, Amy A. Zenger, and Cinthia Gannett, another faculty (Gannett)/graduate student pair (Tirabassi and Zenger), describe their journey from "innocence" into "experience" as their writing center underwent structural and administrative changes that caused them to examine, evaluate, and rethink the roles of graduate student administrators.

Part II: Between: The Ways Graduate Students Challenge Writing Center Theory and Practice

Helen Snively begins Part II by describing a non-traditional writing center at Harvard's graduate school of education. Working in a writing center for graduate students run by graduate students, Snively often found that her tutors and clients perceived their writing center in ways similar to clients and tutors in more traditional centers. Through extensive use of interviews with tutors and clients, Snively provides examples of the ways in which writing centers can benefit graduate students at every stage of the writing process, even when that process is applied to in-depth research and writing projects like theses and dissertations.

While Snively suggests that graduate student clients have many of the same needs as undergraduate clients, having a graduate student cadre of tutors can complicate more traditional notions of tutor training. In chapter seven, Christopher LeCluyse and Sue Mendelsohn discuss the ways in which the traditional weekly staff meeting failed to meet the professional development needs of their graduate student writing center staff. Turning to classical rhetoric, they suggest that the topoi of classical rhetoric can provide administrators with a framework for training graduate tutors to work effectively with/in the complicated dynamic of "peer" tutoring. LeCluyse and Mendelsohn also believe that effectively training graduate students requires trainers to consider the special interests and professional concerns of graduate students.

Another concern for graduate tutors is the issue of collaboration and non-directiveness in tutorials. Seeking to understand how graduate student tutors employ this pedagogy, Brooke Rollins, Trixie G. Smith, and Evelyn Westbrook perform a linguistic analysis of three tutorials conducted by graduate consultants and point to ways in which both tutors and clients work (collude), through their use of language, to make tutorials appear collaborative. This chapter brings to light the great linguistic lengths to which graduate student tutors must go in order to maintain the appearance of non-directiveness in tutorials.

To conclude this section and the collection, in the final chapter, Lucas Niiler examines the relationships graduate students have with his writing center. Using territorialist theory to conceptualize this relationship, Niiler highlights the strategies graduate students use to claim and defend their "territory," offering insight into the ways graduate students at one writing center took control of their liminal space and marked it as their own.

Taken as a whole, the authors in this collection provide an overview of the challenges and rewards that await graduate student clients, tutors, and administrators in the writing center. This collection is intended as a resource not only for graduate students but also for faculty and writing center professionals who work with them. Whether used as a classroom text or a professional development resource, *(E)Merging Identities* provides an opening for sustained conversations about theorizing the work graduate students do in the center as well as foregrounds the professional, academic, and personal stakes for graduate students in this environment.

This collection is an important benchmark in writing center studies because it highlights the fact that as writing centers become more and more a part of academic life, graduate students have and will continue to play increasingly central roles in running, staffing, and using writing centers.

Works Cited

Anson, Chris, and Carol Rutz. "Graduate Students, Writing Programs, and Consensus-Based Management: Collaboration in the Face of Disciplinary Ideology." *WPA* 21.2/3 (1998): 106–120.

Conroy, Thomas, Neal Lerner, and Pamela Siska. "Graduate Students as Writing Tutors: Role Conflict and the Nature of Professionalization." *Weaving Knowledge Together: Writing Centers and Collaboration.* Ed. Carol Peterson Haviland, Maria Notarangelo, Lene Whitley-Putz, and Thia Wolf. Emmitsburg, MD: NWCA Press, 1998. 128–150.

Eckerle, Julie, Karen Rowan, and Shevaun Watson. "When the Administrator is a Graduate Student." *The Writing Center Resource Manual.* 2nd ed. Ed. Bobbie Bayliss Silk. Emmitsburg, MD: NWCA, 2001. Section IV.8.

Fontaine, Sheryl. "Revising Administrative Models and Questioning the Value of Appointing Graduate Student WPAs." *Foregrounding Ethical Awareness in Composition and English Studies.* Ed. Sheryl Fontaine and Susan Hunter. Portsmouth, NH: Boynton/Cook, 1998. 83–92.

"Future Perfect: Administrative Work and the Professionalization of Graduate Students." Rhetoric Review 21 (2002): 40–87.

Harris, Muriel. "Talking in the Middle: Why Writers Need Writing Tutors." *College English* 57 (1995): 27–41.

Jackson, Rebecca, Carrie Leverenz, and Joe Law. "(Re)Shaping the Profession: Graduate Courses in Writing Center Theory, Practice, and Administration." *The Center Will Hold: Critical Perspectives on Writing Center Scholarship.* Ed. Michael Pemberton and Joyce Kinkead. Logan, UT: Utah State UP, 2003. 130–150.

Latterell, Catherine. "Defining Roles for Graduate Students in Writing Program Administration: Balancing Pragmatic Needs with a Postmodern Ethics of Action." *WPA Journal* 27.1/2 (2003): 23–39.

Leverenz, Carrie Shively. "Graduate Students in the Writing Center: Confronting the Cult of (Non)Expertise." *The Politics of Writing Centers.* Ed. Jane Nelson and Kathy Evertz. Portsmouth, NH: Boynton/Cook, 2001. 50–61.

Lunsford, Andrea. "Collaboration, Control, and the Idea of a Writing Center." *Writing Center Journal* 12.1 (1991): 3–10.

Mick, Connie Snyder. "'Little Teachers,' Big Students: Graduate Students as Tutors and the Future of Writing Center Theory." *Writing Center Journal* 20.1 (1999): 33–50.

Miller, Scott, Brenda Jo Brueggemann, Bennis Blue, and Deneen Shepherd. "Present Perfect and Future Imperfect: Results of a National Survey of Graduate Students in Rhetoric and Composition Programs." College Composition and Communication 48 (1997): 392–409.

Powell, Katrina, Cassandra Mach, Peggy O'Neill, and Brian Huot. "Graduate Students Negotiating Multiple Literacies as Writing Program Administrators: An Example of Collaborative Reflection." *Dialogue* 6 (2000): 82–110.

Sunstein, Bonnie. "Moveable Feasts, Liminal Spaces: Writing Centers and the State of In-Betweenness." *Writing Center Journal* 18.2 (1998): 7–26.

Welch, Nancy. "Migrant Rationalities: Graduate Students and the Idea of Authority in the Writing Center." *Writing Center Journal* 16.1 (1995): 5–23.

PART I

Betwixt:

The Complexities of Graduate Student Life in the Writing Center

Just Between Me and Me:

A Letter to Myself About Being
a Graduate Student Tutor and Administrator

Michael Mattison

"The gap between us becomes a potential space."

-NANCY WELCH

Dear Mike:

I know it might seem strange to write a letter to an earlier version of myself (never mind the question of postage), but if there's a chance of this letter reaching you and helping you think through some of the issues you'll soon face, then it's worth it. You are about to begin your graduate career, and a big part of that career will involve writing centers. Trust me; you won't think of writing centers in very much detail at first: writing centers provide an add-on to your teaching assistantship, a chance for a little extra money. But you'll discover that you enjoy the work, and you'll find yourself focusing more and more on writing center theory and practice. Eventually you'll even move into an administrative position. Writing centers, in short, will become central to your life. The catch, though, is that you won't always feel so centered about your work. In fact, you'll feel more often like you're caught in the middle—in the middle between being a teacher and tutor and between being a student and an administrator. It can be an uncomfortable feeling, and one not often talked about in the literature on writing centers and/or graduate work in English.

That's why I'm writing.

I'm not going to spend time talking about tutoring in general. Tutoring is a tough job, with a lot of baggage. As Jerome Rabow points out in *Tutoring Matters*, "Fear, anxiety, and insecurity are intrinsic to tutoring. Intricate situations and emotionally taxing incidents can make tutors not only feel helpless, but even a threat to the educational progress of their tutees" (2). There is much that's been written about handling such feelings, and you'll read it.

What you won't necessarily read about is how the fear, anxiety, and insecurity can be complicated by the fact that you are a graduate student and a graduate teaching assistant (TA) at that.

Being a TA puts you in that strange space between teacher and student, authorized to teach a first-year composition class on your own but still taking graduate classes from others. This dual teacher-student identity brings up what Brian Bly calls the "fundamental conflict" for TAs "between the position of authority they possess as composition professors and the lack of authority inherent in their roles as students in a graduate program" (2). Your dual status will accentuate the uncertainties you have about your ability as a teacher: you're going to wonder quite often if you're qualified to teach a writing course and will just as often question the credentials of whoever decided you could. It is much easier being a student because you know the role: you're accustomed to writing, not to helping others write. And to have to *grade* writing?! That's a dilemma.

In part, it is the confusion and doubt about your teaching qualifications and your worry about evaluating students that influences your decision to go into the writing center. You've heard a little about the writing center—how the tutors work one-on-one with students, talking about papers and writing and establishing a relationship between writer and writer not between evaluator and writer—and the writing center sounds like a place where you might avoid any conflict of authority. A tutor, as Muriel Harris suggests, also occupies a middle space, but that space is different from being an evaluator; a tutor is "a middle person . . . who inhabits a world somewhere between student and teacher" (27–28). Harris's middle position is a more positive one than that which Bly describes, and Harris says that "tutors can work effectively with students in ways that teachers can not" because of their different positions on the "academic ladder" (28). You believe you're not going to have to evaluate writing so much as communicate about it: "Tutors are thus other than teachers in that they inhabit a middle ground where their role is that of translator or interpreter, turning teacher language into student language" (37).

But you learn that your middle ground is rather unsteady because of your role as a TA. An undergraduate peer tutor can be influenced by what *she might write* for the assignment; you, on the other hand, can be influenced by what *you want your students to write*. It's a subtle difference perhaps, but one worth exploring.

There are articles that address issues of authority in the writing center (Cogie; Fletcher; Trimbur), and Jane Cogie—who examines a consultation between a graduate tutor and undergraduate student—warns that you'll need to be "wary of inequities" that exist between tutor and tutee, "differences in academic status, availability of situated knowledge, the predisposition to hierarchical learning, as well as issues of gender and age" (48). But, in most discussions about authority, including Cogie's, the intricacies of how tutoring can be shaped by "differences in academic status" are not examined in detail, especially for a tutor who simultaneously holds status as a teacher.

For instance, Dave Healy says that tutors "can be present as fellow pilgrims in a way that faculty cannot," echoing Harris's idea about a middle person (21). Then he looks to differentiate between the types of authority held by tutors and teachers. Tutors, for Healy, do not lack authority, but they would seem to be able to shed it when talking with writers: "The advantage tutors have over teachers in this [evaluative] enterprise is that even if students try to invest tutors with authority, tutors can resist that role, while teachers, as long as they give grades, have a harder time shedding their image as authority figures" (21). This image sounds perfect for a tutor-teacher, to be able to step into the writing center, drop your uncomfortable authority at the door, and work with writers in a more equal relationship.

What do you do, though, when a student brings in an assignment that nearly matches one of your own? Remember that you're tutoring *and* teaching this semester, and you're teaching one section of a first-year writing class. There are several other sections offered, and all of the teachers have the same general syllabus and attended the same orientation seminar and teaching workshops as you. You all share a textbook. Sometimes you share assignments, and you're going to find that it's *not* always a matter of adopting another stance as a tutor when a writer brings in a paper that could just as easily have been written for you as a teacher. Can you be a nonauthoritative tutor then? Can you resist efforts to invest you with authority if students know that you do assign and evaluate these types of papers? You are still giving grades to such work, which undercuts Healy's notion of an ideal tutor, one who has "no grade-giving responsibility" and is "in a better position to deflect the question" of what grade a paper would receive (22). How do you deflect that question?

Maybe you'll wind up in the middle again, this time between the role of tutor and what Kenneth Bruffee would call a "monitor," or "surrogate teacher":

> What distinguishes [monitors] from collaborative peer tutors is that
> they are set apart institutionally both by the teachers and administra-
> tors who rely on them and by the students who work with them. . . . As
> a result, they are not regarded, and in many cases do not regard them-
> selves, as sharing fully in the vicissitudes, burdens, and constraints of
> normal student life. (84)

You're not a normal student. You're not really a collaborator with the tutees. You're not a peer. True, the writing center is not asking you to be a monitor, but there is the pull towards that role. As much as you might want to lean towards the student-side of your life and commiserate with the student writers who come in to the center (the majority of whom are undergraduates), you'll be blocked by the fact that you teach. And your relationship with your tutees will be influenced if they know you teach, especially if they are consulting with you about papers for first-year writing.

Healy even details an "unsuccessful" experiment in which undergraduate tutors were also asked to be TAs. They experienced a sense of conflict similar to what you will:

> by having to wear two hats—tutor and TA—[TAs] experienced heightened role conflict. Who are they—extensions of the instructor with a responsibility to espouse her/his party line, or employees of the Center with an obligation to its philosophy and practices? Are they advocates of the curriculum and the instructor, or advocates for their fellow students? (23)

Healy concludes that "students need people and places in their academic lives that are free from the stigma of grades" and that "being able to talk about and work on assignments with people who have no grade-giving power (or interest) is important in helping students develop intrinsic motivations for their studies" (23). Again, though, you have grade-giving power; it has been granted you by the institution, and it's not just a simple matter of dropping it off at the door when you come in to tutor.

So what do you do in your consultations? Do you tell students you are a teacher? Some will ask you outright, so you better think on what you'll say. When a writer brings you a paper for first-year writing, do you tell the writer that you usually evaluate these types of papers? That you have a sense of what other instructors will look for? After all, you went through teacher orientation with the other instructors, and you know all of them. You can direct the students towards the paper that you, as a representative of the evaluating culture, know will probably receive a good grade. You may even have explicit knowledge about one teacher's grading criteria or pet peeves. Should you share that information with students?

Certainly these questions raise ethical concerns, and point to the "hierarchical context" that Irene Clark and Dave Healy describe, in which a tutor "might assume an unethically dominant role in creating and developing a text" (250). All tutors need to question how directive they might be in their writing center work, but the question is especially pointed for you given your academic status. You're caught, more than other tutors, between a pedagogical version of Scylla and Charybdis (think back to your Greek mythology class in high school). Sometimes you want to take Jeff Brooks's advice and become the (absolute) minimalist tutor in order to make certain that your role as teacher does not assert itself in a session; other times you feel the pull of Linda Shamoon and Deborah Burns's "master class" image, and you look to display "rhetorical processes in action" and provide "interpretive options for students" by talking about how you would respond to such a work given your status as TA ("Critique" 146). You can use your grade-giving powers for good.

To further complicate the issue, what if you are asked by a student to work on a paper that has received comments from one of your fellow instructors? What if they are comments you don't agree with? As Healy suggests, "Tutors, who see assignments and instructors' comments on papers and who hear students' complaints about particular teachers, are in a position to challenge the instructors' judgment and competence" (25). Do you raise such a challenge in front of a student? Can this be a moment to follow Cynthia Haynes-Burton's advice and "create a space for students to talk about their writing outside of the classroom and hearing of the teacher" (115)? Of course, if you do, you can easily help to create the "envy, mistrust, and misunderstanding between residents of the classroom and the center" that Healy mentions (25). Or, if you decide not to take on the teacher's comments directly but feel the comments are unhelpful, how do you talk about them without indicating that you would have responded differently or given the paper a different grade?

What about the next time you see that teacher in the office? Or at a graduate party? Or in class? Will those handwritten comments ("Awk!" "Vague!") flash in your mind? Will you think the other teacher awkward and vague herself because of them? Will you be tempted to make red circles over the party invitation you receive because that's what you saw all over a student's paper? Will you accept the invitation given your peer's grading habits? When talking about Milton in your graduate seminar, will you silently berate another student for having so much to say in this forum while leaving a student paper unmarked and the student confused as to the reasons for her grade? Will the quick wit of a promising Shakespeare scholar seem mean and sarcastic when directed towards a young writer? You, as a tutor, have access to your peers' pedagogical work in ways that others in your circle do not. Should what you discover in a tutoring session affect your relationship with other teachers? At the extreme, could you ever turn in a fellow graduate student for what you consider unsound or sloppy pedagogical practices?

I don't mean to heap all this on you at once, and I hope I'm not scaring you off from your interest in the center. But I do want you to be aware of all the complexity that comes with being a graduate tutor and teacher. What exactly is the relationship between your classroom and the writing center? Healy notes that tutors stand "apart from the classroom" and thus "provide a means of interrogating academic hierarchy [because they] provide an audience whose relationship to a student's writing is not governed by the same kind of 'oughtness' as is the instructor's" (20). But you are not apart from the classroom, and any interrogation you do will be directed, in part, towards yourself. You help create some of the "oughtness," and the duality between classroom and center is a duality in you. Healy does admit that "writing centers do not constitute an authoritative or evaluative vacuum," yet he does not delve into the complex intermingling of authorities that exist for you (21).

Again, yours is a relatively unexplored position. You're in the middle between two types of middle-ness: the *middle ground* between writer and teacher, which you hope to occupy as a tutor, and the *middle status* between tutor and teacher, which are your two occupations. It's like that song from Stealers Wheel: "Yes, I'm stuck in the middle with you / And I'm wondering what it is I should do."

Along with the uncomfortable feelings of being in the middle, though, comes a lot of learning. You realize that, as a tutor, you do have some insight for students about how people can (and do) respond to papers, and you'll become more comfortable with sharing them. It's not a matter of switching positions so much as acknowledging the multiplicity of positions and noticing the overlaps and connections—and disconnections. Or, in Nancy Welch's terms, you begin exploring the gaps, "lots of gaps—along with a constant, steady attention paid to the experience of contradiction and misfit" (54). Welch's work helps you discover that the uncomfortable position of being in the middle can lead to a better sense of identity: "Identity is created by coming up against the limits of any one mirror, group, or discourse" (57). You create this new identity for yourself, you'll read more about writing centers and begin to "take responsibility for the ways [you] are constituted by [y]our social positions and histories" (Grimm 24). For instance, you're going to have a sense of how students can have difficulty understanding an assignment, and you're going to try and be clearer when writing yours. You'll also pay more attention to the "social and linguistic challenges" Anne DiPardo details because it's impossible for you to make any assumptions about a student's classroom effort after seeing how hard students work on their writing in the center.

In a sense, you'll become more centered as a tutor; you'll take control of that middle position and use it to your and your students' advantage. This will be especially true when you begin work at your next writing center. It, too, is a drop-in center at a large research university, although you'll occasionally have scheduled appointments with a single writer over the course of a semester. Like before, you're also going to be teaching a first-year writing course, so you remain a middle-middle person, but again, you are also becoming more conscious of your positions. You're a more accomplished and reflective tutor. And teacher. And student. Your identities begin to complement one another.

But then, as those positions are coming together, you're going to find yourself in yet another middle space because you're going to accept the position of assistant director of the writing center. That decision will make you an administrator while still a graduate student, and if you thought the student-teacher combination was tricky, just wait until this one.

Again, I'm not trying to scare you, but I want you to be aware of what's coming. When you become assistant director, you take on an authority role that asks you to supervise tutors, some of whom are other graduate students.

You are involved with scheduling their hours, keeping track of their tutoring sessions, talking with them about tutoring practices, and maintaining a professional, well-respected writing center. Those may sound like simple requests, but the balancing act they'll force you into is an extreme one.

For instance, what are you going to do if a graduate tutor, someone you know well and are friendly with, is late once or twice for tutoring sessions? You need to mention it, certainly. And you will, politely. But what if he apologizes to you, then smiles and says, "You know how it is?" Do you nod and say, "Yes, I do," and hope he will shape up? Do you make sure he's scheduled with another tutor so that the center is not left unattended? Do you buy him a watch? As an administrator, you've been given the responsibility of making sure this writing center is a productive resource for students. As a graduate student, you have a social life that is intertwined with those who work in the center. These dual roles are not without conflict.

In fact, your dual roles of student and administrator can pull you in opposite directions. You hear (and occasionally) contribute to conversations about the administrators in the writing program. You know graduate students have complaints and concerns about scheduled meetings, required paperwork, enforced classroom practices, and requests for reflective work aimed at promoting pedagogical growth. There is, at times, an "us vs. them" mentality between the graduate students and the writing program administrators, and your administrative position in the writing center brings you very close to being one of "them." How hardline can you become in your requests for professional behavior before your fellow graduate students begin rolling their eyes at you and making comments about your uptightness?

You'll encounter even more difficult situations when confronting other tutors' pedagogical approaches. Your second writing center also aims to conduct student-centered, facilitative tutorials, relying on a lot of questions from tutors and emphasizing that a student should make changes to her own paper. What happens, then, if you see a tutoring session in which another graduate tutor reads a student's paper silently to herself and then proceeds to rewrite sections of the paper without consulting the student? Do you interrupt the session, perhaps confusing and upsetting the student? Do you conference with the tutor afterwards, asking her how she approaches her tutoring conferences and why she has adopted those directive methods? What if she says she knows what's best for student writers—she realizes they need help in using certain academic conventions—and doesn't concern herself with the writing center policies if she doesn't agree with them? Do you fire her? Plead with her? Ignore her? Change the policies?

Will it change your response if you often encounter this tutor and her fiancé at social gatherings? That you'll most likely be invited to their wedding? Will they look kindly upon a tutoring handbook as a wedding present? You will be forced to ask—again and again—how the personal affects the professional. Your first instinct will usually be to avoid the whole question, to consider giving up one or the other—the administrative post or the social interaction with others.

There are other options, and they again involve reflecting on the multiple roles you inhabit and how best to balance them. Stephen Jukuri and W. J. Williamson talk about administering a writing program, not a writing center, but there are some overlapping concerns:

> Graduate student administrators. . . seem to find themselves in any number of ill-defined positions, ranging from spy to helper, to "reachable" expert, to God on earth, or at times, to intimate confidant. The negotiation of these multiple positionings is always an individual challenge, because each [TA] seems to have a different "take" on who you are supposed to be. (106)

Not only are *you* going to be deciding what position(s) you hold, *other people* will have expectations about your responsibilities: "[O]ne of the greatest difficulties [for a TA] is understanding what any particular individual expects of you, and how they will react when you conduct yourself and define your work somewhat differently from those expectations" (109).

For instance, when you talk to the first tutor mentioned above about being late, he expects you to be a friend and fellow student, something like a confidant. Reminding him about the importance of punctuality positions you as someone else—not God, probably, but more of an anal-retentive archangel—as does suggesting that he might not want to continue as a tutor the next semester if he will not be able to come on time. It's fairly easy to write the words that draw up this scene for you, but imagine standing there in front of him, your eyes not quite able to meet his and your words not quite sounding precisely like they did when you practiced this small speech in your office. You do practice for this new role. You try out the voice you think is necessary for different situations—sounding firm but friendly, diplomatic and still sympathetic.

In this particular case, the issue is resolved as your fellow tutor decides not to come back, citing too many other obligations, and so the two of you do not have to renegotiate the friendship through your interaction as tutor and supervisor. Still, there's a ripple in your relationship. Maybe it's not felt on both sides, but you sense a difference when you pass each other in the halls. You wonder in the back of your mind if he's mad at you or considers you some type of traitor to the graduate student cause. You may actually wonder if he passes you the ball less often in your weekly pick-up basketball game at the gym.

There will be ripples in other relationships, too, as when another tutor-teacher uses writing center time for conferences with students from his course. In all honesty, you wish you could do that; a graduate student's time is limited, and the writing program requires that teachers conference with students. How wonderful it would be to combine that requirement with writing center time, especially during those evening hours early in the semester when few students come in. So yes, you again "know how it is," but you are also responsible for changing "how it is" to something better. A tutor who schedules class conferences during writing center time takes away those appointment slots from other students, and the tutor is being paid twice for the same work. It's another awkward conversation.

Cases like these two, centering on issues of punctuality and proper use of center time, will often stem from the fact that tutors can see writing center work as secondary to either their teaching, their scholarship, or both. Tutoring is not a full-time job for any of the tutors, and, in the hierarchy of their workloads, tutoring comes near the bottom. This is not to say that they are not committed to working with writers or are poor tutors, but they do not prioritize writing center work as you do. In the case of the tutor with a different pedagogical take on tutoring, mentioned earlier, the issue is not about her making the center a priority. She values writing center work, but her work doesn't mesh with the center's idea of tutoring. Again, do you approach her as a boss, with the implication that not changing her methods will result in her dismissal? Or do you try to approach the situation as a teacher, looking to talk out the differences and helping her to understand the reasoning behind the center's pedagogy? Is there a way to be both boss and teacher? Maybe. Will she see you as one or the other regardless of what you do? Possibly. It is a question of power. You have some, but it's certainly not absolute. You almost need to think of your power as a diminishing resource: use a bit at a time, when most necessary. Trying to use up large quantities at once is off-putting to the tutors you work with and to you. Remember, too, that you are the *assistant* director. There are situations that are best handled by the director, and part of being a graduate administrator is learning to recognize when you should turn over a problem to someone with more authority.

In the case of this tutor, you take the roles of teacher and fellow tutor, and it seems as if she regards you as such. You have a good conversation with both of you making valid points, and you believe she now better understands why the center has certain policies and why it is important for all the tutors to follow them. Still, you notice she continues many of her practices in other tutoring sessions. Perhaps you should have been more of a "boss." However, this seems to be a case where you can, and should, talk with the director.

Your relationship with the director will also influence the roles you play. She might ask you to be a spy for her. Not in those terms, of course, but when she asks for an evaluation report on certain tutors, how do you treat the request? There is the pull of different loyalties when offering up your observations about your colleagues, especially as there is no set procedure for evaluations. Your reports are delivered orally, not in written form, and you wonder how your characterizations of certain tutors will be received. What you could really use is a course in writing center administration, but there is none at your university. Such courses are rare and are called a "relatively recent phenomenon" as late as 2003 by Rebecca Jackson, Carrie Leverenz, and Joe Law (131). There is no classroom space for you to learn about and reflect on the work you're doing.

I realize I'm not offering a lot of specific answers in this letter. Of course, you usually think you know best and have trouble taking advice anyway, but there is also no solid guideline for your work. You are, as Atwood Brown terms it, "The Peer Who Isn't a Peer," and you too will often career "back and forth between being a graduate student and an administrator, inhabiting one role or the other, depending on the situation" (121). You're in the middle again, and it's not always comfortable. As before, what can help is to be aware of all the roles you play and reflect on them. Consider how you position yourself, and how others position you. Avoid the siren call to be "God on earth" (nobody will worship at that altar), but remain firm to the goals of the writing center and keep the writers who visit the center as your main priority. That's probably the best advice I can give you.

Guess what else you've got to worry about? Part of your job will be to help advertise the center and to explain to the campus community what the writing center does. You'll write up advertisements for the college radio and television stations, design bookmarks and pamphlets for distribution around campus, write to professors and ask them to inform their students about the center and its benefits, and email departments with requests to link their homepages to the center's website. You'll also work at developing the website, trying to articulate the center's goals and policies for a wide audience. As you will understand by now, the writing center is not a fix-it shop for remedial writers or a drop-off editing service but a place for writers of all abilities to consult about writing. Not everyone, though, is familiar or comfortable with that definition. And when I say everyone, I mean faculty. Even though Muriel Harris explains that those who view writing centers as "unnecessary frills, sucking up funds, space, and personnel to duplicate what goes on in the classroom or to coddle remedial students who shouldn't have been admitted in the first place" are a "diminishing minority" (40), whenever you're in a one-on-one conversation, such a person does not constitute a minority. In fact, if that person is a full professor, you could even say that he is the majority in the conversation. So how do you interact with faculty members?

For instance, when talking to a faculty member who has asked you about the writing center—who wants to know "what you do over there" and why she "should tell her students about it"—do you address her as "doctor" or use her first name? Peter Carino and Katherine Fischer and Muriel Harris have detailed how important our choices of names and metaphors are when considering a writing center/lab/clinic's goals and image, but it's also important for you to think about how you'll name others. If you address this faculty member as "doctor," you might risk presenting yourself and the center in a subordinate role. She'll be reminded of your position on the academic ladder, which could help her think of the writing center as a support service for her, so she will send you the student writers she does not want to deal with. Your use of a title could confirm that status. But if you address her by her first name, you risk offending her because you are not fellow faculty. She could find you presumptuous and might decide not to find out more about the writing center resulting in a lost opportunity for her students and for her.

This might seem a ridiculous example, but I think the question of whether or not to use a first name with a faculty member gets at the heart of your dilemma. With faculty, you're again in the middle, unable to precisely determine the nature of your relationship.

As with the tutors, your relationships will be additionally compromised by the views others might hold about writing center work. Though you encounter few who think the writing center unnecessary, you do talk with those who describe it, at least implicitly, as a prison or hospital (and you'll probably want to read Michael Pemberton's piece about these metaphors, too). For certain faculty, the center is there to help the students (criminals or patients) with a piece of writing (rehabilitate themselves or become well). It will be very difficult for you to counter these images of the center, and I think impossible for you to overtly challenge them. You are, as Shamoon and Burns suggest "without the power or status to alter the general perception that the work [we] are doing is remedial" ("Labor Pains" 69). Furthermore, in this particular institution, the director is not faculty either but a staff member, a designation that also lacks power in the academy. You don't necessarily have a wall of professional support behind you.

Just like before, though, your unusual status can benefit you. You're pushed to reflect on your position and on a host of relationships that affect a writing center: between writing center personnel and faculty in other disciplines; between tutors and writing center administrators; between writing center administrators and writing program administrators. Because you pay so much attention to how all these people interact and where you fit in, you gain a rich understanding of how writing centers are viewed and talked about by various members of the university community. You begin to notice what Jane Nelson and Kathy Evertz term the "terrain of power in which writing centers are located," and you become involved with the "political exchanges that happen during the course of writing-center work" (xi). As before, when you gained a sense of "translating" between teacher language and student language, you gain some facility in translating between writing center language and, well, non-writing center language.

For one thing, when you visit classrooms to talk about the writing center, you learn not to go in blind. Instead, you always request a meeting with the professor sometime during his office hours. During the meeting, you can gain a sense of how he understands the writing center and ask what he hopes you can offer his students. There's sometimes good sense in placing yourself and the center in a "service" role if this opening will allow you a chance to explain what it is your center does and why. In a way, you're following Bonnie Sunstein's advice when she talks about writing centers and the idea of "inbetweenness," which she finds a "position far more powerful than marginal" (8). A lot of the power derives from the ability of writing center folks to redefine ourselves: "When we live in blurred disciplines, hidden between institutional budget lines, we must listen, and speak, and sometimes redefine ourselves to synchronize with the very structures that our centers want to resist" (22). In a conversation with a professor, you can ask what type of assignments he gives his students, how he responds, and what he considers good writing. Then, listen to him. Find places of intersection with writing center work (a goal of clear communication, for instance). You'll have some good conversations if you do, and you can sometimes encourage faculty to redefine themselves and their ideas about writing. In fact, your status as a graduate student might make some faculty more willing to talk about concerns they have about teaching writing or working with writers than they would be with someone closer to their standing. You are, after all, not a peer, and any concerns they share with you are not admissions of incompetence, as they might be with another professor.

So you will have good conversations. You will also, though, discover that there are other conversations that do not go as well, and it's not necessarily a matter of your graduate status. Sometimes, it's a matter of being associated with a writing center. I mentioned earlier that some tutors might not have writing center work at the top of their priority list, and it's fair to say that some universities do not have writing centers as their top priority, either. You need to understand and appreciate the perception others can have about your work, especially should you decide to continue to be involved with a writing center. For instance, if you apply to direct a writing center at a university where you will be classified as English faculty, how will your academic work be compared to that of your colleagues? Even those in the field of composition may ask if you are sure that you want to "do writing center work" (see Singh-Corcoran, this volume).

Now, however, I'm getting into present-day concerns, areas that will require a letter from a future version of both of us. For you and your graduate situation, I've probably said enough at this point, perhaps too much, and I certainly don't want to give away any more surprises for your future. Nor do I want this letter to dissuade you from taking the tutoring assignment. Yes, you're going to end up in the middle, but you will make your middleness productive; you will see it as a way to become more centered in your teaching, your tutoring, your administrating, and eventually in your research. Lynn Briggs and Meg Woolbright say that writing centers can be "microcosms of pedagogical, textual, and human relations, not on the periphery but at the center of language, literacy, and learning" (x). You'll be there, too. In the center. And you'll learn, as Wendy Bishop did, that writing centers "are often sites of exhilarating educational experiences" (158). Mostly, that's what I wanted to tell you. Making the choice to tutor is worth it. It is absolutely worth it.

And, by the way, put all our money on the Red Sox to win the World Series in 2004. Seriously.

Take care of me,

Mike

Works Cited

Bishop, Wendy. "You Can Take the Girl Out of the Writing Center, But You Can't Take the Writing Center Out of the Girl: Reflections on Sites We Call Centers." *Teaching Lives: Essays and Stories*. Logan, UT: Utah State UP, 1997: 157–166.

Bly, Brian K. "Uneasy Transitions: The Graduate Teaching Assistant in the Composition Program." *In Our Own Voice: Graduate Students Teach Writing*. Ed. Tina Lavonne Good and Leanne B. Warshauer. Boston: Allyn and Bacon, 2000. 2–9.

Briggs, Lynn Craigue, and Meg Woolbright. *Stories from the Center: Connecting Narrative and Theory in the Writing Center*. Urbana: NCTE, 2000.

Brooks, Jeff. "Minimalist Tutoring: Making the Student Do All the Work." *The Writing Lab Newsletter* 15.6 (1991): 1–4.

Brown, Johanna Atwood. "The Peer Who Isn't a Peer: Authority and the Graduate Student Administrator." *Kitchen Cooks, Plate Twirlers, and Troubadours: Writing Program Administrators Tell Their Stories*. Ed. Diana George. Portsmouth: Boynton/Cook, 1999. 120–126.

Bruffee, Kenneth A. *Collaborative Learning: Higher Education, Interdependence, and the Authority of Knowledge*. Baltimore: Johns Hopkins UP, 1993.

Carino, Peter. "What Do We Talk About When We Talk About Our Metaphors: A Cultural Critique of Clinic, Lab, and Center." *The Writing Center Journal* 13.1 (1992): 31–42.

Clark, Irene L., and Dave Healy. "Are Writing Centers Ethical?" *The Allyn and Bacon Guide to Writing Center Theory and Practice*. Ed. Robert W. Barnett and Jacob S. Blumner. Boston: Allyn and Bacon, 2001. 242–259.

Cogie, Jane. "Peer Tutoring: Keeping the Contradiction Productive." *The Politics of Writing Centers*. Ed. Jane Nelson and Kathy Evertz. Portsmouth: Boynton/Cook, 2001. 37–49.

DiPardo, Anne. " 'Whispers of Coming and Going': Lessons from Fannie." *Landmark Essays on Writing Centers*. Ed. Christina Murphy and Joe Law. Davis, CA: Hermagoras, 1995. 211–226.

Fischer, Katherine M., and Muriel Harris. "Fill 'er Up, Pass the Band-Aids, Center the Margin, and Praise the Lord: Mixing Metaphors in the Writing Lab." *The Politics of Writing Centers*. Ed. Jane Nelson and Kathy Evertz. Portsmouth: Boynton/Cook, 2001. 23–36.

Fletcher, David C. "On the Issue of Authority." *Dynamics of the Writing Conference: Social and Cognitive Interaction*. Ed. Thomas Flynn and Mary King. Urbana: NCTE, 1993. 41–50.

Grimm, Nancy Maloney. *Good Intentions: Writing Center Work for Postmodern Times*. Portsmouth: Boynton/Cook, 1999.

Harris, Muriel. "Talking in the Middle: Why Writers Need Writing Tutors." *College English* 57.1 (1995): 27–42.

Haynes-Burton, Cynthia. " 'Hanging Your Alias on Their Scene': Writing Centers, Graffiti, and Style." *Writing Center Journal* 14.2 (1994): 112–125.

Healy, Dave. "A Defense of Dualism: The Writing Center and the Classroom." *The Writing Center Journal* 14.1 (1993): 16–29.

Jackson, Rebecca, Carrie Leverenz, and Joe Law. "(RE)shaping the Profession: Graduate Courses in Writing Center Theory, Practice, and Administration." *The Center Will Hold: Critical Perspectives on Writing Center Scholarship.* Ed. Michael A. Pemberton and Joyce Kinkead. Logan, UT: Utah State UP, 2003. 130–150.

Jukuri, Stephen Davenport, and W.J. Williamson. "How to Be a Wishy-Washy Graduate Student WPA, or Undefined by Overdetermined: The Positioning of Graduate Student WPAs." *Kitchen Cooks, Plate Twirlers, and Troubadours: Writing Program Administrators Tell Their Stories.* Ed. Diana George. Portsmouth: Boynton/Cook, 1999. 105–119.

Nelson, Jane, and Kathy Evertz, eds. *The Politics of Writing Centers.* Portsmouth: Boynton/Cook, 2001.

North, Stephen. "The Idea of a Writing Center." *College English* 46 (1984): 433–446.

Pemberton, Michael. "The Prison, the Hospital, and the Madhouse: Redefining Metaphors for the Writing Center." *The Writing Lab Newsletter* 17.1 (1992): 11–16.

Rabow, Jerome, Tiffani Chin, and Nima Fahimian. *Tutoring Matters: Everything You Always Wanted to Know About How to Tutor.* Philadelphia: Temple UP, 1999.

Shamoon, Linda K., and Deborah H. Burns. "A Critique of Pure Tutoring." *The Writing Center Journal* 15.2 (1995): 134–151.

_____. "Labor Pains: A Political Analysis of Writing Center Tutoring." *The Politics of Writing Centers.* Eds. Jane Nelson and Kathy Evertz. Portsmouth: Boynton/Cook, 2001. 62–73.

Stealers Wheel. "Stuck in the Middle With You." *Stealers Wheel.* Lemon Records, 1973.

Sunstein, Bonnie S. "Moveable Feasts, Liminal Spaces: Writing Centers and the State of In-Betweenness." *The Writing Center Journal* 18.2 (1998): 7–26.

Trimbur, John. "Peer Tutoring: A Contradiction in Terms?" *The Writing Center Journal* 7.2 (1987): 21–28.

Welch, Nancy. "Playing with Reality: Writing Centers after the Mirror Stage." *College Composition and Communication* 51 (1999): 51–69.

CHAPTER 2

You're Either a Scholar or an Administrator, Make Your Choice:

Preparing Graduate Students for Writing Center Administration

Nathalie Singh-Corcoran

Shortly before my comprehensive exams, one of my committee members asked me what my plans were after the Ph.D., where I saw myself. When I told him that I *saw myself* directing a writing center, he shifted in his chair uncomfortably and issued a vague warning. He didn't exactly discourage me from pursuing a career in writing centers, but he did tell me that if I wanted to be considered a *scholar* and not *just an administrator* (his words), my future research needed to consider more than writing centers. I got a similar reaction from one of the University of Arizona's English Conference key-note speakers: "Why do you want to direct a writing center?" she said. "It's such a low-status job."

Elizabeth Boquet offers a similar anecdote in "Disciplinary Action: Writing Center Work and the Making of a Researcher." When she tells her dissertation committee that she wants to focus on writing centers, they warn her that her choice will limit her professional career. She might find a position as a writing center specialist but would be "passed over" for any general composition/rhetoric positions. They also tell her that "writing centers tend to be the worst of all composition jobs: temporary, underpaid, overworked, vulnerable," that she will have difficulty publishing her work because of its "limited appeal," and that none of her colleagues will really understand it (25).

In my situation, the irony is that both of those who warned me have published widely and have had prominent careers in writing program and writing center administration. One could assume that because they have had relative success in their areas, they would encourage others to follow similar career paths. Or maybe there is nothing ironic about their statements at all. Maybe because they've endured particular hardships as administrators, they do not want others to suffer the same burden. The warnings and hesitations are not unique to either my own or Boquet's experiences. Writing center scholars have been writing for many years about the common perceptions of their work as low status and unscholarly. Given aversions to writing center work in the academy, why would anyone want to pursue a career in writing centers? I cannot speak for all those involved in writing centers, but I can say that what attracts me—human interaction, attention to written and oral communication, and collaboration—resonates with many others. And because writing centers are such rich sites, sites that embody rhetoric and pedagogy, those who suggest that writing center work is perilous do not dissuade me from pursuing my interests; they incite me. I want to know how such negative perceptions affect the career paths of those who might seek writing center administrative positions.

As new PhDs are being increasingly asked to perform administrative roles, my inquiry seems especially timely. In 1998, 33% of all composition/rhetoric positions (the highest percentage listed among the specializations in the field) were within writing program administration, writing across or within the disciplines, and writing center directing (Stygall 386). The number has since grown. Theresa Enos reports that the October 2000 *JIL* listed sixty-two administrative positions, or roughly 34% percent of the total jobs in composition/rhetoric, and there were between thirty and forty additional administrative positions or positions which required administrative experience posted on the *WPA Listserv* (63). It appears, then, that while many in the field may devalue administrative positions like writing center directing, a growing need for administrators is emerging across college and university campuses. But if attitudes about writing center directing are negative, how is composition/rhetoric, as a field, preparing its graduates to take on directing jobs? In this essay, I consider both field-wide and institutional attitudes towards administration and discuss how these attitudes—implicit and explicit—dissuade graduate students from pursuing academic careers in writing center administration. I also explore how these attitudes may slowly be changing because of the field's employment trends and recent moves made by graduate programs.

Discipline, Scholarship, and Administration: The Shape of the Field

I frame my discussion around three key terms: *discipline, scholarship,* and *administration*. These terms call attention to institutional assumptions that create tensions between writing centers and the field of composition/rhetoric and position writing center work as low in status and unscholarly. *Discipline* and *scholarship* are also terms of indoctrination. Conceptions of these terms shape graduate students' actions, attitudes, and behaviors. The terms inevitably raise issues that are important for composition/rhetoric as well as writing centers' future.

Discipline and Scholarship

On one level, a discipline is a branch of study under which we receive training. But disciplines are also enclosed, highly organized, hierarchical arrangements through which our actions and behaviors are controlled. As academics, we are devotees to a particular order. Jim Corder calls a discipline a tribe, a group to which we give our allegiance, a group that "provides us a way of knowing, seeing, and taking experience" (305). As a discipline, composition/rhetoric often seems vast and without territory. Scholars within it focus on areas as diverse as science, technology, literature, cultural studies, literacy, intellectual property, creative non-fiction. Writing centers as members of composition/rhetoric's domain participate in its boundarylessness, as centers do not subscribe to any one particular brand of pedagogy or theory. Because centers are ill-defined, scholars like Boquet question how there can be any large-scale writing center community (*Noise* 30). However, because composition/rhetoric and writing centers situate work around recurring concerns such as discourse, language, communication, practice, pedagogy, and service, they assert themselves as members of a legitimate academic community.

Writing centers share composition/rhetoric's institutionally marginal status. As many scholars have noted (Connors; Crowley; R. Miller; T. Miller), college composition began as a site of remediation, a space in which students were to make up for the short-comings of their earlier literacy education. While these scholars and others have done much to legitimize composition studies, it has not escaped its century-old stigma as low status work. Writing centers share a similar history and present. Early writing centers were designed to assist underprepared writers. (Bouquet, "Our Little Secret"; Carino). They were service units supplementing students' courses, including first-year composition. Center workers have also attempted to reposition writing centers as a space for play (Boquet, "Our Little Secret" 56) or a viable learning community outside of the classroom (Riley 140). But like composition, they sustain an unfavorable reputation.

Disciplines legitimize themselves through scholarship, and they have specific discursive conventions that govern publishable scholarship. In part because of composition/rhetoric's historical ties to literature programs, some compositionists find themselves operating within a system that privileges more traditional forms of scholarship—historical, theoretical, and empirical—but denigrates practice-oriented scholarship (Briggs and Woolbright; Haviland, et al.; North). The preferred and traditional forms of research and scholarship lend prestige and authority to the field, while a teacher's scholarship about her experiences in the writing classroom may hold less intellectual merit, especially outside of composition/rhetoric. Values about scholarship are often implicit. For example, journals like *College Composition and Communication (CCC), College English,* and *Rhetoric Review* do not explicitly discourage writers from submitting practitioner-oriented texts, but we do not often see this kind of scholarship within their pages. As Richard McNabb argues in his *Composition Studies* article, "Making the Gesture: Graduate Student Submissions and the Expectation of Journal Referees," if someone in the field wants her or his arguments to become validated or accredited, she or he must "shift authority away from everyday professional practices, that is, the material sites of one's activities—classrooms, department hallways, conferences—and into a structured realm of epistemological and methodological frameworks" (11). In other words, a journal will more likely accept a submission if it emerges "from disciplined inquiry" as opposed to personal experience (12). McNabb writes his article for graduate students, and he tells his readership that those who choose to write narratives about teaching are often considered novice scholars.

The hierarchy of publishable scholarship and McNabb's advice do not bode well for writing centers, but they do shed light on the absence of writing center scholarship in some of the field's major journals as well as disciplinary attitudes about writing center work. For the five year period 2001–2006 *College English* did not publish any articles that specifically address writing center concerns. *CCC* published one in its February 2001 edition, but the article, "Centering in on Professional Choices" by Muriel Harris, was an invited submission.[1] The absence of writing center articles suggests two possible conclusions: 1) no articles pertaining to writing centers were submitted to either of the journals or 2) all of the writing center articles submitted were rejected. It is possible that no writing center articles were submitted to either of the journals. Writing center scholars have their own forums in which they can present their work, namely *The Writing Lab Newsletter* and *The Writing Center Journal.* It is, however, also entirely possible that *CCC* and *College English* rejected writing center articles because much writing center scholarship is experience-based. *The Writing Lab Newsletter* consistently publishes practice-oriented, how-to texts: how-to establish a center, how-to promote a center, how-to create a safe and welcoming atmosphere for tutors and clients. And many *Writing Center Journal* articles are written in the first person; the writers tell their stories. The following openings from the Fall/Winter 2002 and Spring/Summer 2004 editions serve as evidence of this common writing center device:

- From Susan Blau, John Hall and Sarah Sparks', "Guilt-Free Tutoring: Rethinking How We Tutor Non-Native English Speakers" — "The frustration level at a recent writing center staff meeting rose with the first mention of tutoring non-native-English speaking (NEES) stu-

---

[1] *CCC* recently published Neal Lerner's "Rejecting the Remedial Brand: The Rise and Fall of the Dartmouth Writing Clinic."

dents. 'I try so hard to stick to the guidelines we learned, but it's so frustrating,' said Bliase one of the writing fellows. Neil, another tutor agreed. 'It's like being caught in a drain. I circle and circle it, trying to avoid it, but by the end of the session, I always get sucked into line editing'" (23).

- From Margaret Weaver's "Censoring What Tutor's Clothing Says: First Amendment Rights/Writes Within a Tutorial Space" — "One of the tutors working in our Writing Center showed up for work last semester in a T-shirt with 'fuck' plastered in large letters across the back. Throughout the day, several tutors and students sought me out to express how offended they were by his shirt. I took the initiative to seek out this particular tutor late in the day. 'Several people have expressed concern about your shirt,' I began. Before I could complete my sentence, though, he responded, 'Well I can wear whatever I want. Freedom of Speech, you know'" (19).

Arguably, by McNabb's design, writing center scholarship like the above is considered amateurish because it uses narrative; it argues from personal experience. His observations are especially significant given the increasing demands for graduate students to publish before they receive their degrees. Publications will help us secure tenure-track positions and that reality necessitates that we become aware of what counts as knowledge in the field and what does not. We are subtly warned that writing centers are dubious sites of serious scholarship.

Administration

When we couple conceptions of writing center scholarship with institutional perceptions of *administration,* my final key term, the issues become even more complex. As others have noted (Enos; T. Miller; Stygall) new PhDs are being increasingly asked to take on administrative roles. But within academia, faculty and administrators are often at odds. David Schwalm calls the two "culturally antithetical" (127). Faculty are "rewarded for intellectual independence, unconventional approaches, [and] intellectual troublemaking [. . .] Their strength lies in analysis and critique, in identifying and complicating problems rather than developing solutions" (127). Whereas administrators must "reconcile competing interests and demands in ways that are certain to be unsatisfactory to many or most involved. And though administrators are interested in clearly defined problems, they are also charged with finding solutions—the most satisfactory available—and moving on to the next problem" (127–28). Schwalm argues that in order to become a successful administrator, one must give up his or her faculty values (130). Abandonment is no doubt met with some resistance. Even though the market shows a growing need for faculty/administrators in composition/rhetoric, during our graduate careers we learn that the institution hierarchically arranges the kinds of work we do. When faculty are asked by their colleagues what they are "working on," they mention their research and up-coming publications and not their committee work or their administrative duties. Their service activities do not hold intellectual currency. The underlying assumption is that academicians advance the discipline, while administrators manage or direct the affairs of the institution. An administrator's task is not to make knowledge.

Graduate students are largely trained to become faculty, to become scholars, and not administrators or service workers. When graduate students decide to specialize in administration, their decision may eventually compromise their academic status, especially if they choose to administer a writing center. Margaret J. Marshall speaks to these concerns when she illustrates the problems that writing center directors face in asserting their administrative work as scholarship. She argues that department colleagues and central administration have difficulty understanding the "intellectual dimensions" of the director's work. Directors compose annual reports that describe "major projects undertaken, the statistics of usage, and the plans for the following year. . . [They] compose or revise mission statements, put oral traditions into the written form of policy manuals, or create tutoring handbooks for new staff members" (77). The list is only a small portion of what directors actually do, but such work is "frequently overlooked when the time comes to evaluate" the director for continuing status, tenure, or promotion (77). Writing center directors continually face barriers that affect their status and the general status of writing center work.

And status is important; it provides power, recognition, and stability, but many writing center directors lack academic status. According to a recent survey conducted by Valerie Balester and James McDonald, only about half of all directors have doctoral degrees (63). Only 17% of their positions are tenure track and most are designated "staff, professional staff, administrator, or academic professional" rather than faculty (67). Some have even gone as far to suggest that a writing center directing position is altogether non-academic. In a *Chronicle of Higher Education* article, located in its "Career Network" section, Al Campbell, a new PhD, suggests 15 alternative "non-academic" careers for those who do not wish to pursue traditional faculty positions. He lists "writing center administrator" among them. He presents and explores various career options because he is a self-proclaimed, failed academic. Because he links writing centers to his own scholarly shortcomings, he perpetuates the idea that writing center work is academically trivial, and it is designed for people who, like Campbell, show a general disinterest in scholarship.

The institution and each academic discipline suggest appropriate modes of behavior from their members; writing center administrative work, however, often falls outside of what institutions and many disciplines deem to be appropriate. Some composition/rhetoric graduate programs are making attempts to change this paradigm. These programs have created administrative internships and courses that move towards the validation of administrative work as scholarly work (see, for example, Ryan and Zimmerelli; Tirabassi, Zenger, and Gannett, this volume). In general, however, most graduate programs do not offer much in the way of writing center administration specialization. Those that do offer it in two forms: administrative internships and courses in writing program and writing center administration. According to Stuart Brown, Rebecca Jackson, and Theresa Enos's 1999 survey of composition/rhetoric doctoral programs, of the sixty-five programs, roughly nineteen offered writing center administrative internships. Graduate students in these positions manage staff, maintain records on writing center operations, coordinate outreach efforts to other departments and liaisons with writing programs, participate in writing across the curriculum initiatives, tutor, train tutors, promote, and advertise the center. Their activities only differ slightly from the director's in that interns generally do not deal with budgetary issues.

Internships can greatly benefit graduate students. Daphne Desser and Darin Payne suggest that internships can help establish and maintain administrative positions as "ethical intellectual work" (90), that they empower students to apply theories they learn in their coursework; they allow students to explore different specializations in the field, and they help with the student's marketability (90). Students in writing center administrative positions receive practical/hands-on experience, but because they are not usually given opportunities to reflect on their practices as assistant directors, the positions themselves perpetuate the idea that a directing position is strictly managerial. As Desser and Payne warn, unless the positions enable graduate students to apply theory to practice and critically reflect on their roles "through dialogues, writing assignments, and other structured means" (92), they will become drudge work and sites of exploitation. Because faculty may not have time and the institution may not have the funds to devote to the administration of a writing center, the position may be parceled out to graduate students: an ever-growing source of cheap labor.

A graduate seminar devoted to administration is one possible solution to the above problems. To date, about a dozen programs offer courses in writing program administration (Enos 62). These seminars focus on larger program administration, but often students have the option of concentrating their course projects on related aspects like writing center administration (White). Approximately five programs offer specific courses in writing center administration. Rebecca Jackson, Carrie Leverenz, and Joe Law's "(Re)Shaping the Profession: Graduate Courses in Writing Center Theory and Practice" outlines the curriculum of three of these courses: at Wright State, Florida State and New Mexico State. The seminars focus on issues such as the pragmatics of administration (managing budgets and keeping records) and the politics of directing a center, and are designed to "encourage students to think and act like writing center professionals" (141).

Unfortunately neither writing program nor writing center administration courses are part of most schools' core curriculum. Purdue is the exception. Students in the Purdue program have the option of specializing in administration, and as part of that specialization, they must take four courses in administration, one of which is a WPA seminar. The goals of this particular course are similar to other writing center administrative courses—to prepare graduate students for their future administrative/scholarly careers. Linda Bergmann teaches the class, and she requires that students complete five projects: they can choose to observe tutoring sessions, write conference proposals and book reviews, compile annotated bibliographies, and participate in committee work for the school's on-line writing lab (Bergmann). Students who participate in the course are encouraged to try a variety of projects from the practical to the theoretical. In this sense, Bergmann's course offers the ideal: it validates writing center work as a site of serious scholarly inquiry; it allows students to participate in writing center work without the possibility of exploitation; and it encourages students to reflect on the writing center and its role at their institution, composition/rhetoric, and the academy. However, due to budgetary constraints and even the lack of faculty expertise in writing center administration, it would be unrealistic for me to suggest that a course like Purdue's could exist in all composition/rhetoric graduate programs.

There are, however, other opportunities for graduate students to reflect upon administrative work, such as faculty and graduate student collaborations on administrative scholarship. During my tenure as a graduate student at the University of Arizona, the faculty repeatedly invited graduate students to participate in writing program research projects and to co-author articles pertaining to writing program and writing center administration. Regardless of what form it takes, it is important that graduate student work in writing centers is validated and valued and that graduate students have opportunities to apply what they have learned in their studies.

Conclusion

How can writing center work gain more disciplinary and institutional footing? Some have suggested that writing center scholars make their work more theoretical and less narrative—that as scholars, we conform to disciplinary conventions because theorizing lends credibility. But this solution is inadequate because writing centers exist amid narrative: they are places where storytelling and storymaking happen. Stories draw people to writing centers. Others suggest that we reposition writing center administration. The WPA's policy statement on "Evaluating the Intellectual Work of Writing Administration" suggests that work is considered intellectual if it, among other things, "requires disciplinary knowledge available only to an expert trained in or conversant with a particular field" (513). As Margaret Marshall argues, "If writing centers are to be kept viable as sites for intellectual work, they need a regular influx of composition scholars with intellectual projects centered on such diverse issues as teacher education, disciplinary writing practices, community literacy, rhetorical history" (83). Writing center workers need opportunities to participate in meaningful intellectual work. At the same time, institutionally specific work has its own value and is as significant as work that deepens the field. Administrators must develop arguments that count and uphold values that are worth working for.

When I began graduate school in 1998, I was the only incoming student (out of nine) who had any previous writing center experience. Of the seven members in the 2004 incoming class, five had worked in writing centers, most as tutors, but a couple had been co-directors. Many of us were introduced to the field through the writing center, and we chose composition/rhetoric graduate programs because of the promise that we could continue the writing center work we found so valuable. The numbers in my program, and I am certain, the numbers in many other programs, indicate that graduate students want to pursue the scholarship of administration, and because of the growing need for WPAs and writing center directors, we can expect that administration will continue to be a significant portion of compositionists' work. This means that the field is changing, maybe too slowly for some. But English studies at-large must also confront the harsh reality that funding for the humanities is dwindling, and therefore, the discipline will need to take notice of service and pedagogy and acknowledge their academic currency.

Works Cited

Balester, Valerie, and James McDonald. "A View of Status and Working Conditions: Relations Between Writing Program and Writing Center Directors." *Writing Program Administration* 24.3 (2001): 59–82.

Bergmann, Linda. "Re: Questions re: your writing center course." E-mail to author. 11 Aug. 2003.

Blau, Susan, John Hall, and Sarah Sparks. "Guilt Free Tutoring: Rethinking How We Tutor Non-Native English Speakers." *The Writing Center Journal* 23.1 (2002): 23–44.

Boquet, Elizabeth. "Disciplinary Action: Writing Center Work and the Making of a Researcher." *Writing Center Research: Extending the Conversation.* Ed. Paula Gillespie, Alice Gillam, Lady Falls Brown, and Byron Stay, Mahwah, NJ: Lawrence Erlbaum. 2002. 23–38.

_____. *Noise from the Writing Center.* Logan, Utah: Utah State UP, 2002.

_____. "Our Little Secret: A History of Writing Centers, Pre- to Post-open Admissions." *The Allyn and Bacon Guide to Writing Center Theory and Practice.* Ed. Robert W. Barnett and Jacob S. Blumner. Boston: Allyn and Bacon, 2001. 41–60.

Briggs, Lynn Craigue, and Meg Woolbright. "Introducton: Reflections on Editing." *Stories from the Center.* Ed. Lynn Craigue Briggs and Meg Woolbright. Urbana, IL: NCTE. ix–xvi.

Brown, Stuart C., Rebecca Jackson, and Theresa Enos. "The Arrival of Rhetoric in the Twenty First Century: The 1999 Survey of Doctoral Programs in Rhetoric." *Rhetoric Review* 18 (2000): 233–374.

Campbell, Al. "Dizzy With Alternate Careers." *Chronicle of Higher Education.* 25 July 2003. <http://chronicle.com/jobs/2003/07/2003072501c.htm>.

Carino, Peter. "What Do We Talk About When We Talk About Our Metaphors: A Cultural Critique of Clinic, Lab, and Center." *Writing Center Journal* 13.1 (1992): 31–43.

Connors, Robert. *Composition-Rhetoric: Backgrounds, Theory, and Pedagogy.* Pittsburgh: Pittsburgh UP, 1997.

Corder, Jim. "Hunting for Ethos Where They Say it Can't Be Found." *Rhetoric Review* 7 (1989): 299–315.

Crowley, Sharon. *Composition in the University: Historical and Polemical Essays.* Pittsburgh: Pittsburgh UP, 1998.

Desser, Daphne, and Darrin Payne. "Writing Program Administration Internships." *The Writing Program Administrator's Resource: A Guide to Reflective Institutional Practice.* Ed. Stuart C. Brown and Theresa Enos. Mahwah, NJ: Lawrence Erlbaum, 2002. 89–100.

Enos, Theresa. "Reflexive Professional Development: Getting Disciplined in Writing Program Administration." *The Writing Program Administrator's Resource: A Guide to Reflective Institutional Practice.* Ed. Stuart C. Brown and Theresa Enos. Mahwah, NJ: Lawrence Erlbaum, 2002. 59–70.

"Evaluating the Intellectual Work of Writing Administration." *Council of Writing Program Administrators.* 1998. <http://www.wpacouncil.org/positions/intellectualwork.html>.

Harris, Muriel. "Centering in on Professional Choices." *CCC* 52.3 (2001): 429–440.

Haviland, Carol Peterson, Maria Notarangelo, Lene Whitley-Putz, and Thia Wolf. "Introduction." *Weaving Knowledge Together: Writing Center and Collaboration.* Ed. Carol Peterson Haviland, Maria Natarangelo, Lene Whitley-Putz, and Thia Wolf. Emmitsburg, MD: NWCA Press, 1998. 7–12.

Jackson, Rebecca, Carrie Leverenz, and Joe Law. "(RE)Shaping the Profession: Graduate Courses in Writing Center Theory, Practice, and Administration." *The Center Will Hold: Critical Perspectives on Writing Center Scholarship.* Ed. Michael Pemberton and Joyce Kinkead. Logan, UT: Utah State UP, 2003. 131–50.

Lerner, Neal. "Rejecting the Remedial Brand: The Rise and Fall of the Dartmouth Writing Clinic." *College Composition and Communication* 59 (2007): 13–35.

Marshall, Margaret J. "Sites for (Invisible) Intellectual Work." *The Politics of Writing Centers.* Ed. Jane Nelson and Kathy Evertz. Boynton/Cook, 2001. 75–83.

McNabb, Richard. "Making the Gesture: Graduate Student Submissions and the Expectation of Journal Referees." *Composition Studies* 29.1 (2001): 10–26.

Miller, Richard. *As if Learning Mattered.* Ithaca: Cornell UP, 1998.

Miller, Thomas P. *The Formation of College English: Rhetoric and Belles Lettres in the British Cultural Provinces.* Pittsburgh: Pittsburgh UP, 1997.

North, Stephen. *The Making of Knowledge in Composition: Portrait of an Emerging Field.* Portsmouth, NH: Heinemann, 1987.

Riley, Terrance. "The Unpromising Future of Writing Centers." *The Allyn and Bacon Guide to Writing Center Theory and Practice.* Ed. Robert W. Barnett and Jacob S. Blumner. Boston: Allyn and Bacon, 2001. 139–52.

Schwalm, David. "Writing Program Administration as Preparation for an Administrative Career." *The Writing Program Administrator's Resource: A Guide to Reflective Institutional Practice.* Ed. Stuart C. Brown and Theresa Enos. Mahwah, NJ: Lawrence Erlbaum, 2002. 125–36.

Stygall, Gail. "At the Century's End: The Job Market in Rhetoric and Composition." *Rhetoric Review* 18 (2000): 375–402.

Weaver, Margaret. "Censoring What a Tutor's Clothing Says: First Amendment Rights/Writes Within a Tutorial Space." *The Writing Center Journal* 24.2 (2004): 19–36.

White, Edward M. "Teaching Graduate Courses in Writing Program Administration." *The Writing Program Administrators Resource.* Ed. Stuart Brown and Theresa Enos. Mahwah, NJ: Lawrence Erlbaum, 2002. 101–112.

CHAPTER 3

The Tale of a Position Statement:

Finding a Voice for the Graduate Student Administrator in Writing Center Discourse

Julie Eckerle, Karen Rowan,
and Shevaun Watson

In the years since the International Writing Center Association (IWCA) Executive Board endorsed the "Statement on Graduate Student Writing Center Administration" in 2001,[1] we have kept our ears to the ground, waiting to hear how—or if—the writing center community put the position statement to work. Happily, we have learned that several members of the community, graduate student administrators (GSAs) and faculty/staff directors alike, are reading the position statement and finding it useful. Here we list a few examples:[2]

- One GSA bemoans the fact that the writing center's graduate staff members are paid several hundred dollars (approximately 22%) less per semester than graduate students who teach classes. Since the position statement argues that GSAs should earn no less than graduate assistants with classroom assignments, the faculty writing center director is using the statement to challenge the prevailing assumption that writing center work is less demanding than classroom teaching and to raise the pay rate for graduate tutors and administrators in her center.

- A writing center director asks incoming GSAs to read the position statement prior to meeting with her to discuss the GSA's roles and responsibilities because, she says, it helps to set the stage for the year ahead and establishes mutual expectations. The director expects GSAs to have a significant role in the writing center and gives each GSA the opportunity to pursue a project that both interests her and

---

[1] The full text of the position statement is included in the Appendix to this article.

[2] Unless noted otherwise, the following examples were gathered as part of Rowan's survey and interview research for her dissertation on GSAs and professional development in writing centers. Although the study did not specifically ask questions about the position statement, some participants volunteered this information.

contributes to the writing center. This allows GSAs to be invested in the center without wielding too much control during what is only a one-year position.

- An outgoing GSA describes how she and the writing center director have used the position statement as a guide as they reconfigure the GSA position. As the result of a recent merger between the writing center and the WAC program, the GSA position had become too much work for one graduate student to handle. The director of the merged programs worked with the outgoing GSA and incoming graduate student staff to divide administrative responsibilities among five students. The group discussed the position statement as part of this process, highlighting the statement's emphasis on the need for GSAs' responsibilities to contribute in vital and meaningful ways to the writing center. As a result, the group has worked to ensure that all new GSAs will have the opportunity to work on projects of interest to them in addition to fulfilling their particular administrative duties.

- A former GSA reports that she included the position statement in the writing center's handbook, which serves both as a promotional document for writing center visitors and as a guidebook and historical archive for GSAs. The center director takes seriously the position statement's strong endorsement of mentorship and professional development and works to develop unique collaborative mentoring relationships with each new GSA.

- A former graduate student co-administrator notes that the statement's commitment to GSAs not being the top writing center administrator "makes a great deal of sense" in practice. Though he did not have problems working with or supervising graduate student tutors, the former GSA witnessed instances when a faculty director was able to intervene in conflicts between GSAs and writing center clients who challenged GSAs' authority. The GSA agrees that writing centers need faculty or staff directors who can intervene should such problems arise.

- In at least two cases, undergraduate student administrators have adapted the position statement to address their particular concerns working in administrative roles in writing centers.[3]

---

[3] We learned of these two adaptations through our research on GSAs for "From Graduate Student to Writing Administrator: Substantive Training for a Sustainable Future" in *Culture Shock and the Practice of Profession*, eds. Virginia Anderson and Susan Romano, and from a participant at a 2003 IWCA presentation on the position statement.

This last example of the position statement in practice is particularly apt, given that the GSA position statement was initially modeled on Jeanne Simpson's 1985 "Position Statement on Professional Concerns." According to *Landmark Essays on Writing Centers,* Simpson's statement is a key document in the history of the writing center profession because it articulates appropriate working conditions for writing center directors and thereby provides crucial goals for the writing center community to continue to work toward achieving. Most important, the position statement provides, in Simpson's words, "a 'basis' for negotiation" (58) and an affirmation in writing of the writing center director's worth. Thus, Simpson's statement occupies a significant position in the written record and collective conscience of this profession and continues to live—in at least one incarnation—through our own statement and all the uses directors, GSAs, and undergraduates described here are finding for it.

While it is far too soon to assess the ultimate impact of the "Statement on Graduate Student Writing Center Administration," we take this occasion to reflect on its short history and potential long-term value, including whether it will make its way from printed text to living document or if it will become part of the archive of the profession, a curious but little-used artifact. This is a critical question, for the statement's transition to and longevity as a living document would indicate not only that our initial concerns about the role of GSAs in writing centers were heard but also that the conversation about the work of GSAs continues. The further benefit, we would like to think, would be improved working conditions for GSAs along with enhanced services at the centers in which they work. And yet, we are also cognizant of several factors that may inhibit this goal, including the overarching difficulty of putting position statements to work, the sometimes grim realities of writing centers' status and funding within their home institutions, and the politics of professionalization in the writing center field. Therefore, although our ideas for the graduate student position statement were met with great enthusiasm and support among the writing center community, we also believe that it is essential to keep the statement alive through continued advocacy of graduate student concerns.

We aim for the statement to become what we are calling a "living document." To our minds, such a statement of professional policies and goals is "living" to the extent that members of the field—practitioners, historians, and theorists alike—find it continually useful within their own writing centers and universities. Such a document must be flexible enough to adapt to the infinite variations of centers and the institutions within which they function, but not so elastic as to be worthless across contexts. It should have ongoing practical as well as theoretical and historical value. Simpson's statement, for example, provides a benchmark, or historical point of reference, for how far the field has or has not come in terms of working conditions for writing center directors, and in so doing, it acts as an important link between the past, present, and future of writing centers. Likewise, the graduate student position statement could serve a similar function in our collective sense of writing center history. A living document charts specific policies within theoretical frameworks and historical trajectories that resonate meaningfully with writing center professionals.

In this essay, we weave together our narrative of the genesis of the "Statement on Graduate Student Writing Center Administration" and our analysis of the GSA's role in writing center practice and discourse in order to highlight the need for continued attention to the issues outlined in the statement. We begin by reflecting on the key tensions that emerged during the process of writing, revising, and securing endorsement for the position statement.[4] Next, we analyze the continuing need for the position statement: what purposes does it serve in writing center discourse and in individual writing centers? If the position statement is in fact to become a living document—an integral part of writing center theory and practice—we believe it necessary to acknowledge these tensions and understand what needs the position statement meets; otherwise, of course, whether it lives or dies would be a moot point. Finally, we turn our attention to the position statement itself, considering some of the myriad ways it can be put to work and become a living document.

Idealism and Reality in Writing Centers: Making Room for Graduate Student Administrators

The "Statement on Graduate Student Writing Center Administration" closely follows Simpson's in outlining an ideal set of working conditions. As with the 1985 statement, such ideals are unlikely to be wholly met in any single writing center. The position statement on graduate students, therefore, is intended as a basis from which writing center directors, GSAs, and other concerned faculty and administrators can revise and improve both the professional development and working conditions of GSAs. It contributes to the vitality of writing centers and our professional community in general, as well as to individual graduate students' professional development, by stating explicit goals for achieving greater recognition for graduate administrators. Arriving at this ideal vision of graduate student administrative positions was, as might be expected, a process of negotiation, collaboration, and revision. A variety of issues arose during the vigorous online discussions that shaped the final version of the statement, and we focus here on these tensions because we believe they exist in the writing center community as a whole and

---

[4] For a brief history of our work and of the position statement's development, see "A Thumbnail History of the IWCA Position Statement on Graduate Student Writing Center Administration" on the International Writing Center Association's Web site (http://www.writingcenters.org/gradhistory.htm).

must be attended to if the position statement is to make a lasting impact.

Our effort to increase graduate administrators' visibility within the writing center community has always been collaborative, beginning with a few graduate students and growing into a larger coalition of faculty, staff, and students. Forging common ground among diverse writing center experiences and building consensus around shared interests and concerns were crucial to initiating change. It was always the dynamic interplay between our similarities and differences that propelled our work forward, gave clarity to our goals, and facilitated productive conversations about the statement with IWCA members. In effect, the position statement evolved from our own wish list—a statement of the possibilities we envisioned—into a set of guiding principles for a whole community. The position statement moved, in other words, from one kind of group ownership to another. This shift transpired as an increasingly larger group negotiated the following kinds of issues: making a general statement of ideals relevant and viable for a variety of writing centers and of roles graduate students may fill; fulfilling the desire to foster inclusiveness; and attending to graduate student responsibility and accountability. As the number of stakeholders in the position statement increased, so did the possibilities for and complications of its adoption and implementation.

As mentioned above, one of the primary features of Simpson's statement that we sought to replicate in this one was the attempt to envision an ideal situation for graduate administrators. We believed then, and still do today, that outlining aspects of the ideal is a powerful rhetorical move that achieves two important aims: on the one hand, defining an ideal that highlights the ways in which probably all writing centers struggle in some regard to fully support the work of GSAs, while on the other, providing concrete examples of practices that could substantially improve the experiences of graduate administrators. As conversations about the applicability and viability of the position statement draft continued, we needed to articulate the purpose of focusing on the ideal repeatedly. Many voiced concern that a statement of ideals was impractical, and even potentially off-putting, because it may not be considered widely relevant. If we agreed that writing centers vary greatly in numerous regards and that GSAs fulfilled an equally various number of roles in writing centers, then we were compelled to clarify how a statement could speak meaningfully to such diverse constituents and conditions. We argued that a statement of ideals was, in fact, the only way to bridge those differences of local contexts. To create a more "real" model of practices, one that could somehow account for the myriad differences between centers, was to risk losing the most salient aspects of our original concerns about the work experiences of graduate administrators in the details. Listserv discussions with IWCA board members pushed us to think through this rhetorical move more carefully.

Another concern about a statement of ideal conditions was that the position statement would be perceived or used as an assessment tool. The position statement does have an evaluative quality to it, but we sought to make clear that the spirit of the ideal is reflective self-assessment for center directors, graduate administrators, and other writing center professionals, not punitive or accusatory judgments. When we originally presented our draft statement to the IWCA community, and as we negotiated with board members about revisions and possible adoption, we sought to characterize the position statement as an opportunity for the organization to take leadership on an important issue. We did not want to accuse IWCA or any of our colleagues of needing to remedy a problem; we did not want to discuss failures or poor practices. Instead, we tried to articulate how the organization could build on the widespread general support for graduate administrators by making such support more explicit and institutionalized. This approach made a statement of ideals much more palatable to the board and the general membership.

A related issue that prompted much discussion at workshops, in IWCA meetings, and on the board listserv was the difficulty of not ostracizing, offending, or excluding those constituents in the writing center community who work in direct contradiction to the ideal set of conditions outlined in the statement. For example, we believed it was crucial to be explicit in our support of graduate students occupying an assistant administrative position rather than directing centers themselves, despite the fact that many graduate students do occupy the top administrative position in writing centers across the country. The last thing we wanted to do was to withdraw completely what little support exists for graduate students in those positions. However, we decided, and members concurred, that the principle that graduate students should ideally be mentored in an assistant role was the more important point to make. The qualifications and clarifications of the first point in the final position statement attempt to garner wide support for that set of conditions that best supports graduate students in their dual roles as administrators-in-training and students who need to complete a degree in a timely fashion.

A third point of negotiation that facilitated the statement's adoption was creating a sense of balance between the increased responsibility and the increased accountability of GSAs. Part of the crux of the position statement is our belief that graduate administrators have more meaningful experiences when they have a real stake in the short- and long-term success of a writing center. If graduate administrators are only "paper-pushers," as a good number are, they miss an opportunity to learn first-hand about supervising and administrative decision-making vis-à-vis university structures. Members of the board shared our desire to improve the learning opportunities for graduate administrators, but some worried that more meaningful responsibility was not matched by meaningful accountability. There was concern, in other words, that the position statement encouraged directors to provide graduate students with more training, professional development, and support without asking the students to be more accountable for their actions and decisions within the center. Discussions focused on the degree to which graduate administrators should be protected from the consequences of their actions by the director or some other supervisor. Some members argued that such protection is crucial to the learning and development of graduate administrators, that they should be allowed to make mistakes fairly risk-free. Others, however, urged the board to adopt a position statement that emphasized student accountability, arguing that this environment was equally or even more valuable for real learning to take place. While the final, endorsed position statement embraces the latter position, a debate about this issue continues.[5] This is but one example of the way in which the position statement can prompt useful discussions about teaching and mentoring graduate administrators and indicative of how the position statement can be a living document, one that provokes more debate, initiates more change, and requires more revision.

The Need for a Position Statement

Those who work in writing centers across the country are quick to acknowledge the invaluable role of GSAs. The professional community, in other words, is well aware of the work GSAs do, and countless current faculty directors were GSAs themselves. This accounts in part for the enthusiastic support so many of these directors provided during our development of the position statement. Nonetheless, for a variety of reasons, valuable writing center scholarship on administration and other issues simply fails to consider how advice, testimonials, and theory may or may not apply to the relatively powerless, often transient, and almost certainly less supported, GSA. Consider, for example, that the first edition of *The Writing Center Resource Manual*, an invaluable guide for writing center directors, did not acknowledge the GSA at all.[6]

When we began working together to address issues related to GSAs like ourselves, we took note of a significant gap between writing center practice, according to which graduate students have long played vital roles in the day-to-day operations of writing centers across the country, and writing center discourse, which is notably silent about the GSA, the work s/he does, and the political and practical complexities of the position. Furthermore, while there are exciting trends within rhetoric and composition programs toward expanding administrative opportunities for graduate students and

---

[5] For examples of how this issue plays out in practice, see our case studies of GSAs in writing centers and writing programs in our essay "From Graduate Student to Writing Administrator."

[6] See "When the Administrator is a Graduate Student: Some Suggestions and Concerns" in the Manual's second edition. This chapter grew out of the same proposal to the IWCA that led to the position statement.

even toward providing more substantive training for such students, the latter development is especially inconsistent from program to program and often inadequate (see Eckerle, Rowan, and Watson, "From Graduate Student"). Indeed, it was realizing this disconnect that brought the three of us (all former GSAs) together and that was the primary impetus for our work on the position statement.

It was out of this silence that our work together began. When we met, we did not set out to write a position statement, though we did want to question the silence in the professional discourse about GSAs and give voice to these particular members of the writing center community. As we all know, the working life of a writing center professional of any status can be quite harried, with far more things to do than time to do them. Add to this the GSA's concern with her/his graduate degree, and it is no surprise that this voice is the one to go silent in the less immediate and pressing world of writing center publications, conferences, and other public forums. But this is precisely why this invaluable voice must be heard. Our initial goal, then, was to meet what we saw as a pressing need for GSAs' voices to be heard in the writing center professional discourse so that the experiences of those GSAs and their writing center constituents could be more productive and valuable. The position statement, along with our other publications and conference presentations, has begun this conversation, though we continue to encourage other GSAs and writing center directors to contribute to the discourse.

In the years since the position statement was endorsed and the final version published in the *Writing Center Journal,* we have come to recognize that, in order for the position statement to become a living document and have a lasting influence on the profession, it must go beyond the initial objective we identified and must meet the changing needs of individual GSAs and writing center directors. As our examples at the beginning of this chapter demonstrate, the statement does meet some pragmatic needs, including the ongoing struggle for equity for writing center professionals. Thus, the statement, particularly the items that address the (potential) exploitation of GSAs, offers support for those GSAs and writing center directors who find themselves arguing for more equitable working conditions.

What is perhaps more interesting is how the statement seems to resonate with deeply ingrained writing center commitments to collaborative, ongoing learning and mentorship at all levels. Writing center professionals have long understood that tutors are not in the writing center simply to provide a service, to do their jobs and leave when their shifts end. We understand that tutors are also continuing to learn and develop as writers, thinkers, and tutors/teachers of writing. We understand that in the best-case scenarios, writing center directors provide multiple forms of support and development for tutors. Likewise, the position statement argues that graduate students administrators should be seen as professionals-in-training. While GSAs provide critical administrative support, they are also learning about how writing centers operate within both the institution and the field, as well as realizing how to bring student-centered pedagogies to bear on their work as administrators. Many writing center directors also recognize that working with GSAs can lead to collaborative learning relationships in which they learn from the GSAs even as they teach them. Thus, the position statement has become a useful touchstone for both graduate students and directors as they define GSAs' roles and responsibilities, attending to what they gain from their experiences as well as how writing centers benefit from their service. Thus, though our work began as an effort to fill a gap in writing center discourse, we have come to see that the position statement's ability to meet such needs "on the ground" is critical to its future.

Putting the Position Statement to Work: Toward a Living Document

Throughout this essay, we have noted our intention for our position statement to take on a life of its own as a working document in individual writing centers. At the same time, we are well aware that such position statements, including those as radical and groundbreaking as "Students' Rights to their Own Language" or the Wyoming Resolution, are not easily enacted in local contexts. Each institution, department, writing program, or center must interpret such position statements within the contexts of specific institutional configurations, needs, resources, and constraints. Nevertheless, we adamantly believe that our position statement can be a useful tool for writing center administrators, faculty, and graduate students alike in their efforts to make graduate student administrative positions beneficial for both the centers and the graduate students who serve them. To that end, we offer some suggestions for how the position statement might be put to work by way of supplementing and extending the above examples of how some writing center professionals are already doing just that. Our suggestions are not exhaustive—we look forward to hearing of innovative ways the statement has been used—but we do hope this list is comprehensive enough to spark new ideas.

First, for those GSAs who do want for adequate support and funding, this statement, along with the WPA Statement "Evaluating the Intellectual Work of Administration" and other such documents, can serve as support for an appeal to departmental or institutional powers-that-be. Unfortunately, graduate students are often asked to take on extraordinary responsibilities without adequate support for the work that they do. Items One, Three, and Ten of the "Statement on Graduate Student Writing Center Administration" will be particularly useful to such graduate students. Item One holds that "[g]raduate students should not hold the top or sole administrative position in a writing center..."; as described above, we believe GSAs learn and function best when they hold substantial, but supervised, administrative positions. Item Three contends that GSAs should only hold such positions for a limited time so that such positions do not interfere with students' progress to degree. Finally, Item Ten holds that GSAs"should receive the same or greater compensation as graduate students teaching in the classroom or performing directed research." Each of these principles is premised upon our belief that writing center administration is intellectually demanding and time-consuming work that should be valued and fairly compensated by the institution. As we are well aware, faculty directors continue to make this case on their own behalf to departmental and institutional administrations; we contend that one way to further the quest for equal recognition and compensation for administrative work is to teach graduate students how to make such arguments or, better yet, not let graduate students become accustomed to underfunding and lack of recognition.

Happily, many GSAs enjoy considerably more support from faculty administrators; we suggest that the position statement can offer such faculty and GSAs a useful tool to expand such support and re-envision GSAs' roles in writing centers. For instance, Item Four states that "assistant directorships should have formal, updated job descriptions written or approved by the director." Based on our experiences and research, we know that far too many GSAs start their tenure without a clear sense of what they will be expected to do, what authority they will have within the center (especially where tutors and other staff are concerned), and how they will be evaluated on their performance. For that reason, we are pleased to see that some writing center directors and GSAs are using the position statement as a starting place for conversations about GSAs' roles and responsibilities and for developing formal job descriptions for graduate student administrators. As noted in Item Five, job descriptions should include "responsibilities that are vital to the work and vision of the writing center." Drafting and revising a job description offer faculty and GSAs an occasion to discuss and, perhaps, reframe the role GSAs play in the life of the writing center.

The creation of formal job descriptions provides a basis for implementing Item Nine, formal evaluations of graduate assistant directors from supervisors. Evaluations are an invaluable opportunity for GSAs to get feedback on their performance and provide a context in which they and their supervisors can discuss not only their immediate concerns but also graduate students' future as administrators (or not, as the case may be). But, without a clear and predetermined set of responsibilities, such evaluations may be frustrating, ineffective, or even detrimental to GSAs. Such evaluations, especially when conducted mid-term or mid-year, provide a way for faculty administrators to express concerns they may have about a GSA's performance and to call for changes as necessary to maintain the writing center's services.

In Items Six, Seven, and Eight, the position statement calls attention to the training and professional development of GSAs. Item Six specifically calls for adequate training for administrative positions and offers several possibilities for how such preparation might be accomplished. Because writing centers vary so widely in terms of resources and operations, each writing center will need to develop its own strategies for providing training for new GSAs. Such training will most likely be individualized and on-the-job, supported by regular meetings with a faculty director or supervisor. Training may also be intertwined with on-going professional development and mentorship, as described in Item Seven. Training and mentorship via directed reading, joint research projects, conference presentations and publications, evaluation and feedback, and other means again support both GSAs, who gain a deeper understanding of writing center administration, and the writing center itself, which benefits from a more reflective and informed administrative team (for examples, see Tirabassi, Zenger, and Gannett; Ryan and Zimmerelli, this volume). As Item Eight suggests, GSAs, and the field as a whole, benefit when they have opportunities to attend and/or present papers at conferences. Faculty directors can help graduate students learn how to write proposals for conferences and seek out publication opportunities in forums like *The Writing Lab Newsletter*. They can also teach graduate students how to network at conferences and even on the WCenter listserv. Of course, given the reality of tight budgets, faculty directors may not always be able to provide funding directly to their GSAs; however, they can advise graduate students on how and where to apply for funding from other parts of the institution and they may also know of scholarship opportunities for specific conferences. This kind of guidance helps GSAs become part of the writing center professional community and also provides them with academic survival skills that they will need long after they leave their writing center posts.

Finally, there are as-yet-unforeseen creative ways that this position statement can motivate and inspire writing center professionals. We hope to continue to hear of innovations inspired by our statement. We encourage writing center administrators—faculty, graduate, and even undergraduate— to share their experiences, research, theorizing, and innovations with the writing center community at conferences and in the pages of our professional journals. We also hope that as the writing center community continues its dialogue about important topics such as the professionalization of writing centers, accreditation, and writing center history, it will include the GSA in these conversations.

Works Cited

Eckerle, Julie, Karen Rowan, and Shevaun Watson. "From Graduate Student to Writing Administrator: Substantive Training for a Sustainable Future." *Culture Shock and the Practice of Profession: Training the Next Wave in Rhetoric and Composition.* Ed. Virginia Anderson and Susan Romano. Hampton Press. Forthcoming.

_____. "Graduate Student Writing Center Administrators: Some Concerns and Proposals." *The Writing Lab Newsletter* 25.6 (2001): 4–6.

_____. "IWCA Graduate Student Position Statement." *The Writing Center Journal* 23.1 (2002): 59–61.

_____. "When the Administrator is a Graduate Student: Suggestions and Concerns." *The Writing Center Resource Manual.* 2nd ed. Ed. Bobbie Bayliss Silk. Emmitsburg, MD: NWCA, 2001. Section IV.8.

"Evaluating the Intellectual Work of Writing Administration." *Council of Writing Program Administrators.* 1998.
<http://www.wpacouncil.org/positions/intellectualwork.html>

Rowan, Karen. "A Thumbnail History of the IWCA Position Statement on Graduate Student Writing Center Administration." *International Writing Center Association.* Ed. Clint Gardner. February 2004.
<http://www.writingcenters.org/gradhistory.htm>.

Simpson, Jeanne. "What Lies Ahead for Writing Centers: Position Statement on Professional Concerns." *Landmark Essays on Writing Centers.* Ed. Christina Murphy and Joe Law. Davis, CA: Hermagoras, 1995. 57–61.

Appendix

IWCA Position Statement on Graduate Students Writing Center Administration

1. Graduate students should not hold the top or sole administrative position in a writing center that is affiliated with their graduate institution, but should instead be given supporting writing center administrative roles.

   A. Appropriate titles include assistant director, coordinator, assistant coordinator, writing specialist, etc., depending on local circumstances. Throughout this position statement, we refer to graduate students' administrative positions as "graduate assistant director," but all graduate student administrative roles should be informed by these twelve guidelines, whatever the title.

   B. Although we recognize that assistant director positions are often occupied by staff or faculty administrators and that these employees often face similar concerns as graduate student administrators, this position statement exclusively addresses the employment of graduate students.

   C. This position statement is not intended to suggest that the IWCA does not support graduate students who do hold top administrative positions in writing centers; on the contrary, this position statement suggests an ideal set of conditions for graduate student employment with the intention of improving working conditions for the graduate student directors and writing center work in general.

2. Assistant directorships should be assigned by faculty members or administrators (such as the director) who are intimately familiar with the workings of the writing center. When this is not possible, the director should at least have input into the decision. While the positions should not be limited to students in rhetoric and composition programs, they should be offered first to graduate students who are interested in writing center work and continuing in the field beyond graduate school. An application process is encouraged.

3. Assistant directorships should be limited-term appointments that support students' needs to complete graduate degrees in a timely fashion. Although invaluable training and experience, a graduate student's administrative tenure should never interfere with his/her completion of the degree and advancement to professional life. Whenever possible, therefore, a graduate student's administrative role should complement his/her program of study and professional interests.

4. Assistant directorships should have formal, updated job descriptions written or approved by the director. Assistant directorship should be established within a clearly defined administrative structure so that assistant directors know to whom they are responsible (ideally the director), who they supervise, and exactly what their responsibilities are. If assistant directors are asked to supervise other graduate students, directors should support assistant directors' supervisory and administrative responsibilities. At the same time, graduate assistant directors remain responsible for their supervisory decisions, administrative work, and professional conduct.

5. Graduate assistant directors should be given responsibilities that are vital to the work and vision of the writing center; assistant directorships should not be primarily clerical.

6. Graduate assistant directors should receive adequate training and preparation for the position. This could involve holding writing center roles that lead to the assistant directorship; ongoing training during the assistant directorship; development and use of resource material for graduate administrators; and/or appropriate coursework prior to the assistant directorship. Training is best done with a strong mentorship program. Whenever possible, connections between teaching and writing center work should be discussed.

7. A faculty mentor, ideally the writing center director, should be directly involved with the graduate assistant director's training and development. Mentoring should adjust to the graduate student's particular professional needs and interests, but may include regular meetings, joint projects, reading or research suggestions, modeling of supervision and leadership skills, conference and publication guidance, and regular evaluation and feedback.

8. Graduate assistant directors should be afforded opportunities for research and publication, and they should have access to travel and/or research funds to pursue such opportunities for professional development. While directors should provide mentorship and guidance for individual and/or collaborative projects, graduate assistant directors are accountable for their own participation in research and professional development projects.

9. Graduate assistant directors should receive regular formal evaluations from their supervisors, and these evaluations should be part of their files.

10. Graduate assistant director should receive the same or greater compensation as graduate students teaching in the classroom or performing directed research.

Chapter 4

Mentoring Graduate Students as Assistant Directors:

Complementary Journeys

Leigh Ryan and Lisa Zimmerelli

In the 1997 article, "Present Perfect and Future Imperfect: Results of a National Survey of Graduate Students in Rhetoric and Composition Programs," Scott Miller, Brenda Brueggemann, Bennis Blue, and Deneen M. Shepherd "suggest that rhetoric and composition programs (indeed all graduate programs within English studies) ought to have a well-planned and thorough mentoring program" (405). Five years later, *Rhetoric Review* acknowledged the concerns expressed in this article with a symposium suggesting "the kinds of experiences faculty should be making as part of students' professionalization" (McNabb 40). Many respondents offered their views of the graduate student perspective, articulating the need to provide writing program administrator (WPA) experience at the graduate level to prepare students for WPA work.

Simultaneously, graduate students Julie Eckerle, Karen Rowan, and Shevaun Watson—all involved in writing center work—began drafting what would eventually become the International Writing Centers Association (IWCA) Position Statement on Graduate Student Writing Center Administration (see Eckerle, Rowan, and Watson, this volume). The position statement addresses use (and abuse) of graduate students in administrative positions. They suggest that

> graduate student administrators should occupy an assisting role, and, according to context, have the opportunity to gain administrative experience, participate in tutor training and assessment, contribute to the development of the center and its programs, benefit from the mentorship of an experienced writing center or writing program administrator, and tailor center responsibilities and professional development opportunities to his/her individual needs. (4)

Eckerle, Rowan, and Watson's attention to the role of graduate students in the writing center is both significant and necessary. It is significant because it has

provided graduate students and faculty with a framework for effective graduate student writing center administration; it is necessary because writing
center WPA work is often shadowed by first-year writing WPA work. Indeed,
there is no consideration of the writing center WPA graduate student experience in the *Rhetoric Review* symposium.

This chapter is a tale of graduate student administration in one writing
center evolving from one model of graduate student WPA mentorship. It is
a tale with two perspectives, that of the mentor and that of the mentee. Margaret K. Willard-Traub points out that "[Graduate WPA] experiences…are
capable of yielding important—even crucial—professional and intellectual
insights for those whose careers will extend well into the twenty-first century" (64). Lisa Zimmerelli's WPA journey began with Leigh Ryan's mentorship at the University of Maryland while Lisa served as a graduate
assistant director in the writing center. It was a mentorship that worked well,
to the mutual benefit of mentee, mentor, and the writing center.

A Mentor's Perspective: Leigh

The concept of mentoring comes to us from the Greeks. In *The Odyssey*, the
goddess Athena comes to Odysseus' son, Telemachus, disguised as Mentês
to serve as his advisor. As Telemachus expresses his insecurities, Mentês reassures him. Then, using phrases like "if I were you" and "if you agree," she
skillfully suggests a course of action to deal with his mother's insolent suit-
ors and find his father. Wisdom personified, she praises and again reassures
him before departing.

Michael Galbraith and Patricia Maslin-Ostrowski describe mentoring
as "a process of intellectual, psychological, and affective development based
on meetings of relative frequency scheduled over a reasonably extended
time frame" (136). Michael Galbraith and Norman Cohen characterize the
mentor as a "wise teacher who accompanies, encourages, instructs, challenges, and even confronts the mentee as the mentee is faced with making
decisions and taking actions" (6), while Laurent A. Daloz suggests that "the
kind of challenge that good [mentors] have to offer is the prospect of the
journey itself because we have been there and our charges have not" (26).
Indeed, contemporary literature often portrays the mentee's experience as
a journey, "a useful metaphor because the mentee as learner is considered
to be on a journey of self-development" (Galbraith and Cohen 6). But the
mentor-mentee relationship is a journey for both, one that offers rich opportunities for each to learn, grow, and gain enormous rewards. William
Destler, Provost at the University of Maryland, states that this relationship
is one based on "a fundamental premise—that of equal responsibility and
accountability for both student and mentor."

At the University of Maryland at College Park, the mentoring of graduate students is not only encouraged but emphasized. President Daniel Mote

has commented on mentorship specifically in his state-of-the-campus address, and the Division of Research and Graduate Studies publishes a booklet/website for departments and graduate students entitled "Strengthen Your Graduate Program Through Mentorship." As writing center director, I formally mentor two graduate students who serve as assistant directors. Because of our size (45–60 tutors each semester—a cadre of undergraduate students, graduate students and retired professionals) and a mission statement that commits us not only to tutoring but also to promoting professional activities like presenting at conferences and conducting research, this number of assistant directors works well.

The two assistant directors collectively work approximately twenty-five hours a week. Seldom are both hired at the same time, which allows an experienced person to help familiarize and guide a newly hired one. The English Department requires that one be an English major, but the other may come from any department on campus. (In fact, assistant directors have come from biology, government and politics, history, journalism, education, art, and American Studies.) This arrangement reflects the mission of the writing center for we serve students from all parts of campus. For the few of these assistant directors who will go on to positions in writing program administration, this position offers an introduction to being a WPA. For other students, it offers some academic administrative experience. For all, however, it offers an insider's view of the writing center, one that I hope will benefit other writing centers they may work with.

The first step to making the mentoring relationship work optimally is to choose mentees wisely. Their presence in the writing center needs to contribute to its overall successful operation. Because they are thrust immediately into a supervisory position, they must demonstrate some tutoring/teaching expertise as they oversee consultants; otherwise they have little credibility. Thus I typically hire people who have worked in a writing center and/or have teaching experience.

Galbraith and Cohen explain that for mentees to

> truly benefit from the help offered by a mentoring relationship, they need mentor participation that is based on mutual trust; accurate and reliable information; realistic exploration of their goals, decisions, and options; challenges to their ideas, beliefs, and actions; holistic support (intellectual, psychological, emotional) of their efforts; and encouragement to pursue their dreams. (6)

The fulfillment of such a tall order starts during the interview process, for it is here that we begin to establish what our relationship will be. We talk at length about my expectations and theirs. What do they hope to gain and how do they envision themselves contributing to the writing center?

I make it clear that this venture is cooperative, that while an assistant director may have specific duties like teaching the tutor training course or conducting certain workshops, we—collectively and individually—will be overseeing daily operation. Conveying a clear and accurate sense of what it means to "oversee daily operations" is perhaps most difficult. To my dismay, some assistant directors have interpreted that phrase to mean simply sitting at their desks during assigned hours and dealing with problems when they occur. In reality, it's keeping abreast of the pulse of the writing center and reacting appropriately to both good and not so good occurrences on a daily basis. It's checking to see how busy the evening tutors were and thanking those who coped with excessive demands and reminding a tutor who habitually comes late that his tardiness isn't acceptable. It's also understanding that as "management," sometimes you do extra things, like cover a tutoring session or workshop when a tutor calls in sick at the last minute.

As part of the interview, I want to hear about applicants' backgrounds, professional experiences, philosophies about teaching and tutoring, and, because interpersonal skills are so important, how they deal with people. Our tutors range in age from 18 to 86, and working with this wide age group—from a headstrong young person to an occasionally cantankerous older one—can be difficult at times.

Because we jointly make decisions about policies and problems, plan workshops and proposals and create materials for them, regular communication—both formal and informal—is important. With none of us full-time, we cover the writing center's forty-two hours of operation in a patchwork fashion, and we keep in touch through informal conversations and email. We also maintain a common calendar, where we write down writing center, professional, and significant academic and personal activities. In addition, we connect regularly at a weekly staff meeting, one that usually includes our office manager.

While I generally run these meetings, everyone participates in planning, organizing, deciding, and evaluating. Galbraith and Maslin-Ostrowski underscore the importance of "mentor-mentee dialogues," conversations "noted for collaborative critical thinking and planning, mutual participation in specific goal setting and decision making, shared evaluation regarding the results of actions, and joint reflection on the worth of areas identified for progress" (137). Daloz notes that in addition to material and emotional support, mentors should provide "genuine opportunities" (26); thus I encourage my assistant directors to contribute ideas and to bring needs or problems to our attention. In most cases, rather than make the decisions and delegate duties, I try to ask "should we do this?" or "what ideas do you have?" and "who wants to do what?" whenever it's appropriate. I might add that it is sometimes difficult to recognize when it's appropriate to take charge, and when I should resist the temptation to be directive or adjust my vision of something (a bulletin board, workshop, handout, etc.) because someone else's version may be as good as—or better than—my own. But granting them room to contribute and create means we often end up with good things we might not otherwise have—like a comprehensive handout on personal statements or a successful proposal for an instructional improvement grant.

One of my aims with their administrative activities is to give them some freedom to be in charge, to deal with questions and problems and make decisions, even to make mistakes and learn from them—but with a safety net (me) that they can use if they wish. Assistant directors have worked with tutors who don't fill out report slips as thoroughly as they should, spoken to tutors who are repeatedly late, handled the retired gentleman who was too sympathetic to young students, dealt with the student or teacher who complained about our services, and come up with an improved scheduling procedure for appointments. Sometimes assistant directors seek affirmation about a decision they've already made: when a tutor, who was appearing before the campus judicial board for his involvement in purchasing a keg of beer, asked one assistant director for a letter of reference to use in his case, she sought my advice. When I told her what I would do, her response was "That's what I thought, but I wanted to check."

Because one aspect of mentoring involves "provid[ing] professional networking, counseling, guiding, instructing, modeling, and sponsoring" (Galbraith and Maslin-Ostrowski 138), I also promote professional activities both on our campus and beyond. We typically apply for a small grant each year, conducting pilot studies and/or implementing new activities to improve our services to students. These efforts, for example, established our Grammar Hotline and have created many workshops and materials which we offer to undergraduate and graduate students and to faculty. Such activities enable my assistant directors to participate in writing proposals and overseeing their implementation and budgets. Collectively, we plan and conduct workshops for public school teachers across Maryland; we present (and assist tutors in presenting) at local, regional, and national conferences, and we publish articles collaboratively. Such participation, and my introducing them to my writing center colleagues and bringing them into our professional and social activities, familiarizes graduate students with the values and norms of our profession. Participation in these professional activities helps them to see themselves within the larger academic community and become a part of it.

Finally, as someone who directed the writing center while a graduate student, I know that the stresses of academic life can affect mentees' lives and, consequently, their work. As they cope with tough courses, qualifying and comprehensive exams, theses and dissertations, job searches—and with disruptions to their personal lives like moves, weddings, divorces, and children—I try to be supportive and make reasonable allowances. Often that translates as being a friend and listening; sometimes it means a temporary adjustment of a schedule or workload, like covering their classes or hours.

As professionals, directors/administrators have a responsibility to share their expertise and help the next generations of directors/administrators, but, in doing so, the journey is very much a complementary one. We are, as Daloz notes, "members of the same species as our [mentees]"—"in motion," and sharing a "kinship as travelers" (27). And this mutual journey offers significant benefits for the mentor as well.

One of the best things about a writing center is that it continually changes, which means that the director is always learning, too. New tutors join the staff each semester as experienced ones leave. Computer programs and new workshops are added; old materials are updated; satellite services are established; the budget increases or decreases. The writing center is never the same from one semester to another. With new territory to negotiate continually, allies are invaluable. Incorporating the wisdom and different perspectives of the assistant directors makes me a better director. Their presence makes me think through things more completely, for making a decision or handling a situation also means articulating clearly—for them and for me—how we came to make particular choices. In addition, working collaboratively enables the writing center to pursue some academic activities that might otherwise be put off or be impossible to do. The writing center can undertake larger, more ambitious projects and complete them successfully.

Seeing my assistant directors learn and grow and move on offers enormous satisfaction. It is wonderful to share the joy of their accomplishments and witness their increasing movement into their own professional roles. And it is especially great fun to have a former assistant director take an administrative position in his or her own right. As one of my former assistant directors excitedly put it when he took over directing a writing center, "I have my very own writing center! Just what I've always wanted!" He and I still talk fairly regularly. But really it's different because now we are truly colleagues, and I rather like the role change. Likewise, Lisa Zimmerelli has moved on to be assistant director of an online writing center at the University of Maryland University College. Our professional relationship continues, but on a more collegial level. Recently, we coauthored the fourth edition of my book, *The Bedford Guide for Writing Tutors.* We also continue to present jointly at conferences and recently co-chaired the Mid-Atlantic Writing Centers Association Conference with the Naval Academy.

The mentor-mentee roles that we as writing center directors-assistant directors assume involve both tremendous responsibilities and rewards, but overall, it is a win-win situation. There are precious few of those, and so they must be treasured.

A Mentee's Perspective: Lisa

In "Present Perfect and Future Imperfect," Miller, Brueggemann, Blue, and Shepherd note the disparity between Rhetoric and Composition graduate student satisfaction with mentorship and support *within* a program and their dissatisfaction with awareness and understanding of their discipline *outside* of a particular program (397). As a PhD candidate in Rhetoric and Composition who has recently transitioned from a writing center administrative graduate assistantship to a non-tenure track writing center administrative position at another university, I appreciate their call for mentorship that "achieve[s] a difficult balance between fostering an enriching and welcoming 'present tense' while also being rigorously realistic and honest about the 'future tense'" (404). To be honest, I am not quite sure which tense I am in: I am *presently* ABD with the hopes of doing a tenure-track search in the near future; however, I have also entered that *future*, to a degree, with my current WPA position as the assistant director of the University of Maryland University College Writing Center, a full-time administrative faculty position. I'm in a time warp. But I'm not in this time warp alone.

Like many of the graduate students surveyed by Miller, et al., I feel fortunate to have an array of talented support and mentorship at the University of Maryland. However, unlike most of those respondents, I also feel mentored as I attempt to maneuver into my own "future tense" of academia. It was only through my graduate student WPA work that I had the opportunity to be immersed in one version of my future tense; it was only because of my WPA mentor, Leigh Ryan, that I was able to come out the better for it and still interested in writing program administration. Truly effective mentorship extends beyond the particular writing center in which a graduate student WPA gets her start—effective mentorship establishes a relationship that continues to provide support and camaraderie.

To frame my discussion of the significance of mentoring graduate students in the writing center, I will draw on the theories of conversation, contact zones, and collaboration, terms which have become cornerstones in writing center theory and praxis. As a tutor in a writing center and a teacher of composition, I see these theories played out every day—writers and I wrestle together with language and ideas to arrive at meaningful texts. As an assistant director in a writing center, however, the ideas of talk, conflict, and resolution come even more clearly into focus, and these theories frame my experiences as a writing center administrative mentee.

In "Talking in the Middle: Why Writers Need Writing Tutors," Muriel Harris depicts the tutor as both the institutional and intellectual mediator between teacher and student; the tutor is in an ideal position to help the student wade into the sometimes murky—and often scary—waters of academic English. Writing program administration can be just as murky and just as scary, and it certainly requires much conversation. Thus, the mentor/mentee relationship operates in the same sort of liminal space as the tutor/writer relationship. According to Harris, "Writers both need and want discussion that engages them actively with their ideas through talk and permits them to stay in control" (31). Such talk assists writers with the acquisition of "strategic knowledge"— knowledge that "arises out of an individual's recognition of a set of possibilities for action" and comprises a repertoire of strategies for different tasks and purposes (33). Similarly, graduate student WPAs need talk to acquire the strategic knowledge of writing center administration. When I first became Leigh's mentee, my repertoire of strategies was scant, and our daily discussions were paramount in the development of my WPA philosophy and approach.

I became an assistant director of the University of Maryland's writing center in the fall of 2001. I did have a writing center background, but it was limited to my undergraduate tutoring experience in a one-room, one-person operation. I thoroughly enjoyed peer tutoring, but there had been no theory to my method; I had received no training other than the mantra, "Do not edit students' papers." I also had a composition background, but it was limited to three semesters of teaching in the University of Maryland's freshman writing program. In a word, I was green. For the first semester of my assistant directorship, I often felt as though I made no significant contribution to the writing center. I showed up, participated in weekly meetings, and, every once in a while, jotted a brief administrative email to tutors. What I did a lot of, however, was talk. I talked with the tutors about how they had handled "tough" tutoring situations; I talked with my co-assistant directors about how to approach inappropriate conduct in our writing center; mostly, I talked with Leigh. Often, our conversations revolved around writing center professional issues. Leigh would ask my opinion on a potential policy change, or we would strategize ways to get pay raises for our tutors. I would suggest a new writing center-sponsored program, and we would discuss the pros and cons and the logistical concerns of implementing it. However, many hours of conversation were also logged discussing both academic and personal issues. I talked about my seminar papers; she talked about her scholarly connections to a local historical house museum. I shared the dramas of my upcoming wedding; she shared stories about her grandchildren.

Significantly, it was this talk—this open conversation between novice and expert—that helped reveal to me the subtle—and not so subtle—political trappings of WPA work. Margaret Willard-Traub points out that institutional and departmental politics often demand both the unconscious and conscious participation of central administrators, tenured faculty, graduate students and untenured faculty and "impacts the intellectual work of teaching, of curricular development, and of administering writing programs" (63). WPAs cannot escape such political machinations. Indeed, we often need them to get adequate funding, teachers, and support. However, we can make our participation in the political framework of academia more conscious through talk. Mentoring, based on conversation, helps to make power structures visible and enables the graduate student WPA to see more clearly her position in relation to others in the institution. Further, mentoring helps her to reflect, strategize, and—significantly—to act.

Leigh engaged me in talk that enabled me to explore new issues and enter a new discourse community within a safe space. I am sure that I revealed errors in judgment when discussing writing center policy and had serious misperceptions about other administrators, faculty, and colleagues. As we reflected together, Leigh asked me questions and prodded me to explore fully the implications of what I had proposed or stated. She established clear objectives, provided constructive feedback, and appropriately challenged me. Significantly, however, she also gifted me the freedom, control, and time to negotiate my role and contribution to the writing center. Thus, she helped me attain the strategic knowledge necessary for successful writing program administration. Just as a tutor helps a writer interpret what Harris calls "teacher language," Leigh helped me interpret departmental and writing program administrative language. Slowly but surely, I assembled my own repertoire of strategies for dealing with the day-to-day demands of a writing center. By the end of that first semester together, I gained the confidence to move from reflecting and strategizing to action. I planned, wrote, and implemented new policies, tutor training assignments, grants, and WAC projects.

In retrospect, I believe that Leigh allowed me such a slow and easy introduction to our writing center because she wanted me to know it as alive, to understand the diverse energies and commitments that make it tick on a daily basis. She wanted me to know it as a contact zone, a social space, in Mary Louise Pratt's words, "where cultures meet, clash, and grapple with each other" (34). What I have come to discover is that, just as for tutors and writers, the writing center is a contact zone for writing program administrators. We interact with not only the various cultures of our students and tutors but also with the unique cultures of institutions, departments, writing programs, and our shared writing center community. Leigh was the mediator as I struggled to understand the dynamics of these real and imagined communities. Together, we established what Pratt identifies as "ground rules for communication across lines of difference and hierarchy that go beyond politeness but maintain mutual respect" (40). This journey with Leigh amongst and between contact zones was my maiden voyage; in my current position as Assistant Director of the Effective Writing Center at University of Maryland University College, I have depended upon these fundamental navigation skills.

The idea of the graduate student WPA in a contact zone reflects the *Rhetoric Review* "Symposium" participants' consideration of power and authority in academia. According to Roxanne Mountford, "Graduate students need sustained opportunities to reflect upon the nature of power and authority in higher education" (49). The contact zone that Leigh made visible to me was not just a present tense contact zone; it was a contact zone with a history and with a fluidity that suggested no guarantees. As Leigh shared various departmental and institutional histories, I appreciated the fluctuation of power structures, from dean to dean and from state mandate to state mandate. I understood that our writing center and our present was not the norm; indeed there was no WPA norm, and I certainly would not find it when I went on the job market.

The metaphor of the contact zone also applies to my graduate experience overall. My adjustment from a small, liberal arts college with a strong sense of community to a large department in a large research university had been a difficult one. When I decided to move from a literature focus to a rhetoric and composition focus, and when I became a writing center assistant director, I felt an almost palpable difference. I was supported and mentored by faculty who understood, all too well, the importance of guiding graduate students through the contact zone of academia. Several of the *Rhetoric Review* "Symposium" participants stress the role of collaboration in helping graduate students negotiate the WPA contact zone (Duffey, et al. 84). I would argue that the writing center, particularly steeped in the principles of collaboration, offers an ideal opportunity for WPA mentorship.

Leigh emphasized that collaboration was paramount to success in the writing center. She encouraged me to re-conceptualize and design the tutor training course, building on what earlier assistant directors had established. Although we never talked nor met to discuss the course, I considered these former assistant directors my collaborators in this project. Leigh and I—and often another assistant director—presented at conferences together, co-wrote several grants, and created handouts and other resources. Opportunities for collaboration between Leigh and me have only increased since I left the assistant director position. We continue to present together, and we were co-chairs of the Mid-Atlantic Writing Centers Association 2006 Conference. These kinds of collaborative experiences are invaluable because they provide mentees with opportunities to engage in various kinds of WPA work, such as presenting, chairing, and publishing.

Collaboration becomes, clearly, a potentially rich site for mentoring graduate students in WPA work. When I was with the University of Maryland College Park writing center, it made sense to collaborate, to not "recreate the wheel" with each new assistant director, but rather to build on the work of assistant directors before me. However, in retrospect, this was also training for WPA work more generally. As Mountford articulates, collaboration is particularly necessary for writing center administrators; we challenge, negotiate, and synthesize the curricular and pedagogical expectations of writing instructors, freshman writing program directors, and deans and provosts. In the writing center field, collaboration is not just a cushy word for shared work; collaboration is also survival. In my current position, I have written a department mission statement with my colleagues, proposed a new course with my dean, revised an assignment with a computer science professor, and argued for more funding with my director. There are few activities that I do in isolation, and I have learned that to address writing needs across the university, a writing center administrator must "spend most of her time in collaboration with others" (Mountford 44).

When I was a graduate assistant director, the writing center became, to use Andrea Lunsford's famous metaphor, my Burkean Parlor. I was not given prescribed administrative "rules" for the writing center, nor was I expected to know intuitively what was expected and needed of me as a writing center administrator. Rather, Leigh and I—and indeed all the members of our center—arrived together at a shared sense of the writing center and its mission. I often think back on my experiences there as I supervise and mentor my current team of writing advisors. The conversation and collaboration that defined—and continues to define—Leigh's and my mentor/mentee relationship has enabled me to envision a realistic future tense.

Works Cited

Daloz, Laurent A. "Mentors: Teachers Who Make a Difference." *Change* 15.6 (1983): 24–27.

Destler, William. Introduction to *Strengthen Your Graduate Program Through Mentorship*. College Park: University of Maryland, Division of Research and Graduate Studies.

Duffey, Suellynn, Ben Feigert, Vic Mortimer, Jennifer Phegley, and Melinda Turnley. "Conflict, Collaboration, and Authority: Graduate Students and Writing Program Administration." *Rhetoric Review* 21 (2002): 79–87.

Eckerle, Julie, Karen Rowan, and Shevaun Watson. "Graduate Student Writing Center Administrators: Some Concerns and Proposals." *Writing Lab Newsletter* 25.6 (2001): 4–6.

Galbraith, Michael, and Norman Cohen, eds. *Mentoring: New Strategies and Challenges. New Directions in Adult and Continuing Education, No. 66*. San Francisco: Jossey-Bass, Summer 1995.

Galbraith, Michael, and Patricia Maslin-Ostrowski. "The Mentor: Facilitating Out-of-Class Cognitive and Affective Growth." *Teaching Alone, Teaching Together: Transforming the Structure of Teams for Teaching*. Ed. James L. Bess. San Francisco: Jossey-Bass, 2000. 133–150.

Harris, Muriel. "Talking in the Middle: Why Writers Need Writing Tutors." *College English* 57 (1995): 27–42.

Lunsford, Andrea. "Collaboration, Control, and the Idea of a Writing Center." *The Writing Center Journal* 12.1 (1991): 3–10.

McNabb, Richard. "Introduction," "Future Perfect: Administrative Work and the Professionalization of Graduate Students." *Rhetoric Review* 21 (2002): 40–41.

Miller, Scott L., Brenda Jo Brueggemann, Bennis Blue, and Deneen M. Shepherd. "Present Perfect and Future Imperfect: Results of a National Survey of Graduate Students in Rhetoric and Composition Programs." *College Composition and Communication* 48 (1997): 392–409.

Mountford, Roxanne. "From Labor to Middle Management: Graduate Students in Writing Program Administration." *Rhetoric Review* 21 (2002): 41–53.

Pratt, Mary Louise. "Arts of the Contact Zone." *Profession* 91 (1991): 33–40.

Willard-Traub, Margaret K. "Professionalization and the Politics of Subjectivity." *Rhetoric Review* 21 (2002): 61–70.

CHAPTER 5

Songs of Innocence and Experience:

Graduate Student Administrators
Negotiate Positions of Power

Katherine E. Tirabassi, Amy A. Zenger,
and Cinthia Gannett

"Innocence dwells with Wisdom but never with Ignorance"

WILLIAM BLAKE

In this essay, Amy Zenger and Katherine Tirabassi, two former graduate assistant directors in the Connors Writing Center and Writing Across the Curriculum Program at the University of New Hampshire (UNH) and Cinthia Gannett, the former director, discuss our particular journey from innocence into experience as we worked to understand some of the complex and conflicting positions of power that graduate students often occupy as assistant administrators in a university writing center. We "come to terms" with our experience here both by narrating it and by offering a set of insights and commentaries on key issues. These insights emerged for us as we negotiated administrative responsibilities over two years when significant changes in the administration of our writing center brought issues of intellectual and institutional power into clear relief for all three of us.

We have called on several theorists to help us make sense of our specific situation, centering those discussions with the common but useful theme of the move from innocence to experience. Like Nancy Grimm, we have come to believe that

> to locate literacy problems in cultural construction, we must abandon positions of *innocence* [. . .] and come to terms with the political implications of writing center work. We must also pay much more attention to the cultural assumptions that we bring to writing center work. (29) (Italics added).

Losing our innocence was, in this case, a necessary step in the process of becoming more aware of our own tacit assumptions about writing center work and more discerning about how writing centers do their work in the larger political scene of the university.

In particular, we also found ourselves repeatedly turning to Blakean notions of innocence and experience to make meaning out of our exciting but tumultuous work in the writing center at that time. We turn to Blake because he focuses not only on a loss of innocence but also the recovery of wisdom through a fall into experience and into a new kind of understanding of "contraries," or paradoxes, that he calls "organized innocence."[1] We offer his rich poetic metaphor as inspiration and frame for each of the three sections.

We call on Blake, then, as a partial framing metaphor and extend his metaphor to the work of current writing center scholars who also invoke notions of innocence, its loss, and the recovery of what Elizabeth Boquet calls an imaginative form of "hope," rather than naïve optimism: "For the writing center, such imagining involves refusing an identity construction that merely positions the center as a reduplication of the sound of the academy" (141–2). Our experience with the multiple and often contrary academic cultures with which writing centers must engage when graduate students have vital and powerful administrative roles, though difficult, has brought us to a place of organized innocence, a place of hope.

In the most "innocent" of circumstances, the many constituencies—administrative, faculty, and students that power the writing center—from the university provost to the first year writing student—all work together in harmony, and the needs and expectations of the various groups are readily aligned and articulated. The "fall into experience" that occurred for us when we found ourselves caught up in an unexpected shift to a new administrative structure awakened us to what was at stake and made us painfully aware of desires we had for ourselves and for the curriculum. However painful, the fall into experience is also a fall into language, and it has given us a much richer, more fully embodied sense of the many ways that writing centers participate in institutional conversations.

---

[1] In "Songs of Innocence and of Experience: Shewing the Two Contrary States of the Human Soul," Blake offers his vision of human experience in which innocence, a state of simple, trusting, idealistic belief, is overtaken by a darker, more mature vision—a complex, often ambiguous, even world-weary view of life that comes inevitably through the "experience" of experience. The Norton editors M.H. Abrams, et al., define Blake's innocence as "represented by the naïve outlook of the child who believes what he is told by his elders, and takes appearance for reality and the best aspect of things for the whole truth" ("Songs" 1306). Blake's song cycle shows how "the state of innocence needs to yield to that of experience" and that with experience comes insight ("Songs" 1306).

Innocence[2]: A Director Sets the Scene

When the events of this situated narrative and analysis began in 2001, the Connors Writing Center and WAC Program were—at least provisionally—in a state of "innocence." Having weathered nearly ten years of dynamic development and the profound loss of the founding writing center director Dr. Robert Connors in 2000, we all had a sense of having created a strong and resilient infrastructure for an enduring WAC and writing center program at the University of New Hampshire.

Formalized in Academic Senate Legislation from 1995, a strong, well-developed curricular requirement anchored the joint WAC/WC program and ensured a genuine, if modest, funding-base. A Writing Advisory Council was mandated to oversee the program; an undergraduate tutoring course had been developed; we created a thriving writing fellows initiative, began service-learning and outreach collaborations, and provided full consulting support for graduate students and faculty across the curriculum.

Our program harvested the "experience" of many earlier programs and the increasing body of research, theory, and practice to consciously resist the traditional remediative identity and gatekeeping functions often forced on writing centers and writing programs more generally by educational hierarchies (Boquet; Grimm). Drawing on Barbara Walvoord's "The Future of WAC," and Karen Vaught-Alexander's "Situating Writing Centers," we had worked to collaborate with other interested and potentially innovative projects and organizations in the University, including General Education, Preparing Future Faculty, Teaching Excellence, the Partnership for Service Learning, learning communities, and assessment efforts.

From the very beginning, the joint program grew out of the interests and energies of the faculty of the doctoral program in composition/rhetoric in the English Department, and graduate students were seen as instrumental in creating, organizing, consulting, and researching in the program. The very first pilot budget from 1993 created a single course release for the two senior faculty and significant stipends for two graduate students, and, from its inception, the formal program included two full teaching assistantships for PhD students interested in writing center, WAC, and writing program research and administrative work. These two assistantships allowed graduate students to gain administrative experience, participate in serious professional development and research opportunities, and continue graduate work productively—in an effort to help create the productive balance between multiple roles.

---

[2] This section is told primarily from the perspective of the director, though all sections are co-written by all three authors. The "Experience" Section is written primarily from the GSAs' perspective and the final section: "Toward Organized Innocence" is written from our joint perspective.

We also created one of only eight graduate courses in doctoral programs in rhetoric and composition nationally that offered a graduate course on writing center and WAC history, theory, and practice (Jackson, Leverenz, and Law 137). Katherine and Amy had both taken the only iteration of this UNH graduate course offered in 2001, and it served as important preparation for their positions as graduate assistant directors in the WAC/WC program. Indeed, UNH was featured in the *Times Princeton Review Supplement "Best Colleges for You"* (2000) as having one of the leading WAC/WC programs in the country because of its full range of well-developed and well-integrated WAC/WC initiatives.

We believed that we had a realistic view of the writing center's stature in the university, a program well-regarded and endorsed by an administration, which was fairly supportive and informed about general principles of WAC/WC theory and practice. However, we were soon to learn through a series of dramatic events and the subsequent administrative restructuring of the WAC/WC program that key members of the university's administration had a very different vision for the WAC/WC program than we did; our loss of innocence was in our recognition that the administration's vision conflicted so greatly with our own and seemed to shift so quickly over the course of just a few months.

The prompt for this radical set of shifts began when Cinthia took a leave of absence to teach at a college in Maryland, closer to her husband's work. Members of the University Writing Committee and Cinthia urged the Vice Provost for Academic Affairs to hire an interim director with expertise in composition studies to run the writing center and WAC programs during her year-long absence. We offered options for filling the interim post with internal and external people who could continue to steward the program effectively. Instead the Vice Provost chose the director of another university program (a faculty member with no expertise in composition studies) as interim director of WAC/WC and hired two part-time faculty as associate interim directors to administer the day-to-day running of the two programs and report to the interim director.

When the university administration appointed a faculty member with no expertise in writing center work to direct the WAC/WC programs, a manager rather than a disciplinary expert, it was a critical signal that competing institutional agendas were at work. William H. Bergquist's discussion of competing academic subcultures—the collegial, or disciplinary loyalty and faculty autonomy in teaching and scholarship, and the managerial or hierarchical authority and top-down leadership—may help explain the potential conflicts in these two academic models, especially in regards to making decisions about WPA positions. Bergquist's commentary on these two models would prove especially prophetic:

[University] administrators see themselves in control of mission, curriculum, financial funding priorities, and academic personnel. Institutional research, especially empirical designs and quantitative summative evaluations, presumably guide the managerial culture to rational and equitable program decisions. In reality the managerial culture, while valuing such research, may exercise its authority to set its own agenda, leaving faculty and programs feeling powerless and isolated from key decision-making. (qtd. in Vaught-Alexander 124–125)

The academic culture where WPAs, WAC, and writing center directors primarily live, focuses on long term development of the student, the faculty, and the curriculum. Karen Vaught-Alexander argues that such a culture, "a marriage between collegial and managerial cultures, the development culture ...often pleases neither" (125). Given these multiple cultures in the academy, Vaught-Alexander believes that we need to understand that while writing center and WAC program successes are more than "lucky circumstances," "program setbacks" are generally the result of "something other than professional and personal incompetence" (126).

When circumstances left the writing center program vulnerable to the imposition of a managerial agenda, there were a variety of consequences: as director on leave, Cinthia was increasingly excluded from conversations and decision-making, and the Writing Committee also found itself increasingly de-authorized (as we explain below). But the difficulties created by the intersection of competing academic cultures most profoundly affected the graduate assistant directors, made them precarious, exposed, especially vulnerable to professional damage. Importantly, although this consequence was not intended, the managerial directorship also inevitably altered the graduate assistant directors' job descriptions; while the original purpose of these assistant director positions was to allow graduate students to be mentored in these administrative roles and to be provided with professional development experiences, the new directorship model tried to reduce the graduate student positions to a low-level graduate student labor force, performing only the WAC/WC program's daily operational and clerical operations.

For all of us who are engaged in fostering productive roles for graduate students in writing center work, then, these issues deserve additional reflection, analysis, and efforts to address. While this is a specific and situated narrative, our story begins to address more systemic and symptomatic readings of the differences in institutional power and models of pedagogy with regard to writing center work. Our "fall" into the experience of these tacit competing cultural perspectives helps us understand our own loss of innocence not as individual and capricious but in relation to the complex trajectory of particular institutional cultures and their multiple subcultures.

Experience: The Stories of Two Graduate Student Administrators

For Amy and Katherine as graduate student administrators, our new experience, in essence, helped us to see a reality we'd not been privy to until the administrative restructuring. In Blakean terms, we had a "fall into experience." Experience brought us an understanding of how we were seen in our dual roles as graduate students and graduate student administrators and gave us a clarity we could not have had without the administrative changes—a clarity we have learned from and that has allowed us to enlarge our ideas about writing center praxis. Facing administrative changes that we considered incompatible with theory and practice in composition pushed us into articulating disciplinary knowledge not only for ourselves but also for people inside and outside of the field of composition (university and program administrators) who held various positions of power over us.

Before being hired as assistant directors, we had taken courses in WAC and writing center theory and had each worked as consultants in writing centers outside of the University of New Hampshire. Under the supervision and mentorship of Cinthia, during our first year as administrators, we supervised and trained writing consultants, dealt with day-to-day operations, met with faculty about incorporating writing into their curriculum, offered workshops, collaborated on designing formative assessments, initiated several action research and scholarly projects, helped coordinate a speakers' series and new programs, and contributed to policy decisions made by the senior staff. We worked and learned along with Cinthia as she met with faculty and administrators about writing in the disciplines, presented in public forums such as the Faculty Senate, or chaired the University Writing Committee[3] meetings.

Before the appointments to administer the center during the director's leave of absence, we had hoped for an interim administrator who could continue to mentor us as Cinthia had, but both the interim director and the interim associate director of the writing center held PhDs in fields that were not related to composition studies; neither was familiar with the theoretical underpinnings of writing center or WAC work.[4] In this new configuration, we graduate students were placed in the very awkward position of having more expertise in writing center and WAC work but less authority than our supervisors. And that authority would be repeatedly eroded over the year.

---

[3] The University Writing Committee was a body composed of one member representing each of the twelve schools and programs, as well as the director of WAC and the writing center, and members from Academic Affairs, the administrative "home" of these two writing programs.

[4] The interim associate director of WAC did have a doctorate in rhetoric and composition and some experience with writing centers, but she was marginalized in this new power structure from the very beginning. Even so, she was a very important and helpful part of our support network during this difficult time.

As the interim year (2002–2003) began, we were determined to sustain an atmosphere in which open dialogue would allow each member of the new team to be learners as well as teachers. During our first senior staff meeting, the new interim director announced that he wanted to maintain the status quo, continuing the work of the director who was on leave. Despite this claim, it soon became apparent that he had come into the position not as a learner but as a business administrator, hoping to "streamline" current practices, and increase student numbers. We soon discovered that the only measure by which practices in the writing center were to be streamlined was the bottom line, or how a practice could be measured by its presumed cost effectiveness. For example, one of the first decisions the interim director made was to eliminate the writing consultant position designated specifically for an expert in ESL writing because he did not see quantifiable proof in the statistics of the previous year that the position was warranted. This decision haunted the writing center for the rest of that year as we scrambled to find ways to assure those concerned with ESL support that we had adequate resources to support ESL students and to train all of the tutors more extensively in working with second language writers by scheduling additional staff meetings devoted specifically to this topic. Immediately thereafter, the interim director canceled our outreach efforts to support tutoring in five area high schools, saying that this work was beyond the scope of this university writing center's responsibility. Clearly, there was no strong exigency on his part to continue or maintain the status quo.

Instead, the interim director began to initiate a set of new projects which we saw as potentially contrary to the work of our center. First, he suggested that the center should acquire an anti-plagiarism computer program to offer to faculty. Although we responded that offering this program to faculty could represent a service that might cause students to feel as though they were under surveillance and alter the center's relationship to student writers, our concerns were brushed aside. His argument was simply that such a program had the potential to raise the profile of the writing center on campus.[5]

Similarly, the interim director decided to undertake the project of writing a new mission statement for the writing center, though a mission statement already existed. In a memo to the University Writing Committee, the interim director attached a list of priorities for the writing center that highlights his misunderstanding of writing center work through his use of the phrase "students who need remedial instruction in the writing process" to describe the center's primary clientele and purpose. As Stephen North says in "The Idea of a Writing Center," writing center directors expect such misunderstandings about writing center work, even among colleagues, and hope that through education, these misunderstandings can translate into fruitful

---

[5] Although the proposal to adopt an anti-plagiarism computer program was researched, ultimately such a program was not adopted by the Robert J. Connors Writing Center.

conversations about writing center work. The disheartening fact, in our case, was that our interim director, the person entrusted with directing these two vital writing programs, did not understand the work we did nor did he acknowledge the research of composition scholars as a valid basis for developing an understanding of that work. Although he was not a member of the English Department, the focus of North's plaint, our interim director, as one involved with teacher development programs, harbored what North calls a "second layer of ignorance" and a "false sense of knowing" about writing center work (433). His belief in the "remedial," utilitarian nature of the writing center and in the corporate model of administering institutional programs assured him of his qualifications to write a mission statement for the writing center and to ask those of us working in the center day-to-day to mark up his copy to reach a finalized version of the mission statement. We felt that dialogue should accompany such decisions, but the interim director indicated that he would not welcome dialogue; instead, we responded to the request for written changes to his mission statement by writing individual, alternative mission statements that we would later merge. This approach allowed the rest of the senior staff and writing consultants to participate in the discussion about writing a mission statement for the center while accommodating the interim director's decision to develop a new mission statement.

We were seen as increasingly disobedient, transgressive, but we felt strongly about upholding standards and practices commonplace in writing center theory, and we were enacting our beliefs through the process we'd been accustomed to—a democratic discussion. As we noticed the dialogue shutting down and began to question our exclusion from major decisions in the writing center, we found the writing center space changing in ways we no longer recognized. Nedra Reynolds, in *Geographies of Writing: Inhabiting Places and Encountering Difference,* says that "one way to make connections to places from which we feel alienated is to plunge in, spend time there, and figure out what creates and upholds the hardened boundaries or the geographies of exclusion" (158). As we saw ourselves being excluded from administrative decisions, and even from some day-to-day decisions in the writing center, we began to test the new boundaries around us, if only to understand the limits being placed on us. We tried new tactics to open up the dialogue once again, such as raising questions at senior staff meetings, bringing writing center literature into our daily discussions, and consulting external readings and advice from fellow writing center colleagues regionally and nationally, trying to pursue an ethical response to our new situation.

As the semester wore on, despite our efforts, the dialogue continued to shut down and the list of infelicities mounted. We were taken aback when the interim director, at a University Writing Committee meeting discussing the restructuring of the discipline-based writing fellows program asked the assembled faculty, "So what IS a discourse community?" And when Katherine brought the *IWCA Position Statement on Writing Centers* to a Fall 2002 University Writing Committee meeting dedicated to discussing the restructuring of the writing center, the interim director dismissed the document, published in 1985 (Simpson), as "outdated," and the document was not taken up as a standard to consider. Though Katherine later reported that the IWCA President had confirmed the statement was the latest version, the interim director responded that he had conducted his own literature review and was looking into alternate sources, though nothing ever came of that search. We soon found that anything looking like the *public* exercise of expertise on the part of graduate students was rejected.

These changes towards a managerial culture culminated in the moment when the interim director and other administrators decided to pull the joint WAC/WC program apart and turn it into two separate administrative units, which they argued would make both sets of overlapping projects more *efficient*. The University Writing Committee was asked to review and revise the administrative structure of the WAC/ WC program in accord with this specific agenda, and a strong push was initiated to assess writing intensive courses in more quantitative ways. As compositionists, we viewed both of these developments as seriously alarming, especially because neither was informed by consulting experts, even Cinthia; after all, she was the director *on leave,* and any of these changes would impact her directly were she to return to UNH to continue directing the joint program. It began to appear as if the university administration intended to subsume the WAC program under the larger teaching development program at UNH and to shift the writing center away from the busy teaching, researching, and learning site that it had been to merely a remedial place for "fixing" student texts. We began to speak up more in staff meetings, at University Writing Committee Meetings, and in private to try and explain our views of composition and writing across the curriculum and to fight against what we felt were moves that would weaken both programs immeasurably.

The turning point in our fight for the writing center we had known and loved occurred in a moment of silence or, more accurately, of being silenced. We had always served as ad hoc members of the University Writing Committee, in keeping with the view that there should be graduate student representation on the University Writing Committee and that graduate assistant directors are professionals-in-training. During the interim year, we continued this role with the consent of our supervisors and the committee members, participating and offering resources and composition research when the conversation turned to questions of writing theory or writing program administration trends. We contributed to the conversation until the meeting during which our invitation to these meetings was revoked by the interim di-

---

[6] When we were hired as graduate assistant directors, participation in the University Writing Committee was listed on the job description for the graduate assistant directors prior to and during the interim year.

rector.[6] Because other members of the University Writing Committee felt that we had a theoretical perspective to offer that would otherwise be missing from the conversation, however, they requested that we attend a special Writing Committee meeting with the Vice Provost for Academic Affairs—a meeting that would include a discussion of proposed administrative restructurings for the WAC/WC program. When we arrived at the meeting space and sat down, the interim director immediately exerted his power over us by standing up and asking loudly, "What are you two doing here?" One of the Writing Committee members who had invited us immediately explained why she had requested our presence, and, though we'd attended most other writing committee meetings, our director told us we were not members of the committee and commanded us to "Leave now."

The incident itself was over very quickly, but it effectively illuminated several of the issues we had been grappling with over the course of more than one semester. Our eviction from the room that day graphically represented our eviction from the discussion about the administration of these programs. The incident also publicly demonstrated how the interim administrators viewed us. Our eviction from the meeting stunned other faculty who were on the committee or who heard about the incident indirectly. We had tried to describe feelings of being silenced or ignored to concerned members of the University Writing Committee before, but we had the sense that other people only understood what we were experiencing after they had witnessed this exchange.

Cheryl Glenn points out that when "the dominant group in a social hierarchy renders 'inarticulate' subordinate or muted groups," the subordinate group is effectively barred from "the formulation, validation, and circulation of meaning" (25). In the moment that we were silenced, we chose an alternate form of expression—we left the meeting as gracefully as we could in the uncomfortable silence, and we began to see our work situation more clearly. As non-expert administrators, these men were in power, the ones with the rights and privileges, and the ones who could banish their non-credentialed and female employees—the graduate students—from the room. In our staff meetings and other meetings with these men, we were asked for our opinions or, more accurately, asked to confirm their plan for the future of WAC/WC at UNH. When our theoretically informed responses did not support their opinions, we were seen as a threat to the plan and were silenced before we could speak. We saw then the tenuous position we were in; although our positions in the center carried the title assistant director, our position in the university was graduate student. Even though we'd always been treated as colleagues-in-training by the professors in our program, we saw that outside our department, our graduate student position, regardless of our understanding of writing center and WAC theory and practice, rendered us as a non-expert labor force in the eyes of our supervisors, though they themselves had no experience in writing center or WAC work, and we had several years of experience between us.

Toward Organized Innocence: Four Issues of Power in Graduate Student Administration

The programs we helped administer were forcibly shifted away from the leadership and control of compositionists, a shift we perceived as a threat to the well-being of the programs. Our own well-being was also threatened because negotiating the events of those two years compromised our time and energy in ways we could hardly afford, and our work also became profoundly disheartening.

Though we were rendered powerless in certain obvious ways, we realize that, paradoxically, we also retained—and even gained—a sense of agency and investment that might not have been possible without this set of "experiences." The events we experienced forced us to theorize our own roles as graduate students in the writing center and to theorize more generally about the role of administration in fostering writing pedagogies. We continued our work training undergraduate consultants, supporting graduate student writers, and working directly with faculty on their courses and assignments across the curriculum. We worked to sustain the positive culture and work of the center wherever we could, by modeling collaborative practice. Even when we were silenced, we acted as witness to changes that diminished the efficacy of the work. We learned to handle the loss of formal agency by forming new networks and communities for frank conversation and strategic brainstorming.

Through our experiences as program directors and graduate student administrators, we moved, in a Blakean sense, from an innocent view of institutional administrative politics and hierarchies, through our experience of these structures to an "organized innocence," a combination of our idealism and experience leading to more realistic views of the scope of our expertise and influence (obstacles, limitations, and possibilities), of how administrative structural changes could affect the theoretical underpinnings of the writing center, and of future possibilities we could envision for the writing center. In this final section, we will discuss four paradoxes of power, gleaned from our experiences, that we believe graduate student administrators may face as they work in an administrative capacity in a writing center.

The Need for Professional Development

One of the most important insights we gained about our roles was that professional development was crucially important to us and also easy for others to overlook. When we were first hired as graduate assistant directors, the roles we were expected to fulfill had been conceived by Cinthia as a rich mix of work and learning. Each assistantship job description presented a view of graduate assistant directors as professionals-in-training contributing important work—

practical, theoretical, and research-oriented—to the center. This mix of work and learning fits with the IWCA's "Position Statement on Graduate Student Writing Center Administration" #5: "Graduate assistant directors should be given responsibilities that are vital to the work and vision of the writing center; assistant directorships should not be primarily clerical." The roles we were expected to fulfill as graduate assistants changed, however, in the eyes of our new supervisors who viewed our work as a "job" and who preferred to see us as non-experts, providing quantifiable "clerical" labor (twenty hours a week). As debates over the structure of the program intensified, the number of hours we were working became a bone of contention between the factions struggling to control our program (both those who meant to be well-intended towards us and those who were not). But as we navigated arguments about our working hours, we realized that taken by itself "number of hours" was not a meaningful statistic for us. In determining whether the work we were doing was exploitative, we saw the presence (or not) of a professional mentor who could coach us through decision making and introduce us to people and ideas in our field as a much more significant factor. We came to realize that any description of our work as graduate student administrators that did not portray it primarily as a form of professional development diminished support for our effectiveness and for us.

The debate over our job descriptions has led us to argue that graduate students' roles must be represented as inherently paradoxical, as balancing both not knowing and knowing, innocence and experience. We had observed such a paradox in the roles of the graduate students who came to the writing center to work on their writing: the academic contexts in which they were working constructed them as powerful and vulnerable at the same time. As Carrie Leverenz points out, "When graduate students come to the writing center, everyone's expertise is at stake: the graduate student's expertise in a particular discipline, the tutor's expertise in writing and tutoring, and the disciplinary professor's expertise as a teacher-mentor" (51). The graduate student writers we saw in the writing center were powerful as the minds of the future in their chosen fields and in the success of their academic careers, but they felt vulnerable as novices in the eyes of their professors and in navigating unfamiliar territory as writers and thinkers.

Graduate writers visiting the writing center were often dealing with feedback (or critiques) from their professors that, at times, confirmed their imposter syndrome (the feeling that they did not belong in their particular program) and paralyzed their writing even further; they were facing the need to understand and write in a genre they did not know and had never seen before. Because they felt sheltered from the evaluative gaze of their graduate programs, graduate students visiting the writing center were able to rediscover their own writerly agency and felt re-authorized as experts in their fields. Most importantly, however, we needed to value the non-expert aspect of their understanding, as they negotiated language of their field that felt both familiar and unfamiliar, and the need to write in genres that were new and yet required of them.

We experienced similar paradoxes in the positions of power during our second year as graduate student administrators. On one hand, we were elated to have been placed in a position of power that would enable us to enact our developing disciplinary and programmatic understandings in ways that had real consequences for faculty, students, and the whole curriculum. For example, we co-taught the tutor training course, designed discipline-based workshops with and for faculty, developed policies and procedures manuals, participated in university writing committee meetings, and worked with graduate students and faculty on extended writing, research, and curricular projects. Furthermore, the interim administrative structure placed us in the position of having more practical, theoretical, and local knowledge (and also needing to have more) than the people to whom we reported. But descriptions of our jobs primarily in quantified terms, as "number of hours," ignored the inherently paradoxical nature of our roles. Expert mentoring had provided us with a way to "organize" our non-expertise and to maintain a healthy, dynamic interaction between our experienced, expert selves and the parts of us that were inexperienced; mentoring should be a central feature in all graduate assistant directorships (see Ryan and Zimmerelli, this volume).

The Need for Continuity

A second important insight we gained into writing center work was the importance of structuring continuity into our programs. Our situation underscored the inherently transient nature of writing center work. Continuity can, of course, be fostered by creating both graduate assistantships and more permanent faculty/staff positions, thus ensuring that there will be people who know the center's theory, practices and operating procedures and can maintain them from year to year.

However, sometimes even our best efforts to create staffing continuity are disrupted. When the first director of the writing center, Bob Connors, passed away suddenly two years earlier, the center suffered—in many ways—but certainly from the loss of decades of cultural memory. When Cinthia left the center for a year shortly thereafter, the knowledge of the writing center embodied in those who had lived its history began to fade and with this knowledge, the vision that had inspired the writing center's inception. Since writing center work is usually comprised of short-term contacts with students and a transient writing consultant student staff, important histories, words of wisdom, and cautionary tales that reside within the people who work in the writing center can be lost. Our experience was no exception.

Rather than allowing the history of the programs to fade into ignorance, we argued for building in solid administrative structures that could guarantee continuity, help strengthen the writing center in the long run, and protect inexperienced graduate students from being placed in the first line of defense when programs were threatened. The continuity in the historical knowledge of the writing programs was almost entirely lost with the change in leadership and staff at the UNH Writing Center and WAC programs. Administrative decisions also made it less likely that the history of the center would be preserved. In the summer of 2003, the leadership positions of these two writing programs were further downgraded, the main administrative position split into two lesser positions, with the WAC director becoming a faculty associate with a single course release (a faculty member with no expertise in composition studies), and the writing center director becoming a non-tenured, seventy-percent time position. The graduate assistant director positions, previously held by PhD students in composition studies, became "graduate assistants," and those hired were MA students in fields other than composition studies. The graduate assistant position transformed from a mentored position intended as professional development for the graduate student to a simple labor force position; the graduate assistants no longer contributed to the theoretical framework of the writing programs and fulfilled the clerical and presentational needs of the directors, essentially the job that the interim directors of the previous year had envisioned.

We could not prevent those changes, but we could try to preserve the historical record of the center and its work carefully. As Shirley K. Rose has forcefully argued, telling local stories and creating an archive of photographs, reports, and publications is one powerful way to foster a historical identity for the writing center, strengthening both the sense of community in the present and sense of connection with the past.[7] To that end, Cinthia acquired funding to undertake an archive project for the WAC/WC programs. In collaboration with the university archivist and with composition historian John Brereton, we were able to lay the groundwork for a collection that links artifacts and documents from our programs to all of the holdings in the university archive that are relevant to writing and writing instruction at UNH.[8] The Writing Archive we created will provide a record to fill in the parts of the history of the writing programs that were lost in the contentious transition to the new administrative structure. In this sense, the archive represents a form of "organized innocence": creating an archive was a structured and positive response to our experience.

---

[7] In another loss of historical memory, the assistant director of the writing center, who had worked at the writing center for over ten years, resigned her position at the writing center in January 2005.

[8] For an extended discussion about our creation of a writing program archive, see the following reference: Brereton, John C., Cinthia Gannett, Elizabeth Slomba, Katherine E. Tirabassi, and Amy Zenger.

When we recognized that the program we once cherished could not be saved, we felt a sense of urgency to resist its total loss—to preserve a record of its ten-year existence and to hope that this record would serve a future director of this writing center. And, as we have moved to new ventures in our professional careers, we have brought with us this conviction that, as Shirley K. Rose argues, a "functional" writing program archive can serve future writing program administrators in understanding, contextualizing, arguing for, and reshaping current practices in light of historical or even recent past practices of a program" (109).[9]

The Need for Integrity

A third important insight provided to us by our painful experience was that matters of personal and professional integrity can get very complex and confusing when graduate students act as assistant administrators in a writing center because there are so many possible and conflicting allegiances. Although we still shared our opinions and ideas at senior staff meetings and University Writing Committee meetings, we were silenced gradually because we were not being listened to; our suggestions or expressed concerns were not heeded because of our graduate student status and because the theoretical knowledge that we did possess became too dangerous, too incongruent with the plans that our directors had (though we were never told what these plans were).

For example, in a staff meeting during the interim year, our comments suggesting that it would be good for writing center consultants to learn how to be sensitive to their own cultural and racial positions was met with a resounding negation from the interim director: "There is no relation between writing and race!" Although we had begun serious discussions with consultants about race, culture, and writing center work during the previous year and our personal and professional commitments to this work continued, this proclamation abruptly ended the writing center's collective commitment in this area.

Eventually, our silence became *both* imposed and deliberate. Since there were certain forums in which we could no longer speak or were no longer effective speakers, we turned to alternative conversations to voice our concerns. Cheryl Glenn points out that

> Just as a blurted-out statement or an alleged misstatement can reveal us, so can our silence, whether controlled or instinctive. Just as we use words to obfuscate meaning or to buy time, we use silence [. . .]. The question is whether our use of silence is our choice (whether conscious

---

[9] On a positive note in terms of professional development, Amy's work on the archive at UNH supported her own archival research on daily composition themes at Harvard in the late nineteenth-century. And Kate used the archive as the primary source for her dissertation on composition pedagogy in the 1940s.

or unconscious) or that of someone else. (13)

Our being silenced became a choice to remain silent, to listen, and to share our insights with one another—an act of interpreting what we'd heard—and in our informal conversations with other interested, more credentialed speakers who might have a better influence in shaping conversations about the writing programs than we could. In this way, our silence might have implied acquiescence but was actually a form of resistance. Our rhetorical situation called for both silence and speaking out, and we had to find an ethical means to consider our concerns and share them in an environment that was a safe one for us (Glenn).

Like the graduate student writers we had worked with in the writing center, we found that we needed to find spaces away from the watchful eye of our administration where we could work through our understanding of unfamiliar situations and demands. We found these spaces in our regular conversations among the three of us, with other graduate students, with compositionists inside and outside our university (including the associate director of the WAC program), with key faculty from other departments, and with alumni of our graduate program whom we met at conferences and who stayed in touch through email. Our affiliations with the Northeast Writing Center Association (NEWCA) provided a crucial and supportive forum during this time.

We needed these safe spaces (Boquet; Reynolds) away from the current administration in order to take the pulse of the changes that were rapidly altering the mission of the writing center's work. Since we could not trust our interim directors to engage in analytical conversations about theory, nor could we trust that we would be listened to by our superiors, we found that scheduling conversations weekly with one another and with theoretically informed colleagues helped us take stock of ongoing occurrences. These conversations became touchstones for us, allowing us to bring to voice concerns that had remained just below the surface or concerns we didn't know we had until we talked. They helped us sort out the larger institutional forces[10] at work, ethical decisions we needed to make, and the kinds of action that could still make a difference. Although we were silenced, these regular networks let us speak, let us "make noise" as Boquet would say.

---

[10] As long as the theories and practices of the writing center seemed to function in a consonant way, we didn't have an occasion to question each choice that we made as administrators. But as the administration was submitted to restructuring, who and what deserved our allegiance (the people, the ethical stances, the theories, the institutions) got less clear.

The Need for Theory

Finally, and perhaps most important of all, these experiences taught us the value of integrating theory with practice into our work every day. Working with interim supervisors who insisted on the purely "practical" nature of writing center work taught us to believe that the opposite was true: every administrative choice we make—even the most mundane—has a theoretical dimension and theoretical consequences. In our experience of the interim directorship, we saw firsthand how action without theorizing could lead to shifts in a writing center's foundational philosophy. Practices that were altering the theoretical framework that the center had been based on began to creep into daily writing center life. For example, a change as minor as restricting composition teachers from the English Department having access to the photocopier created a new barrier to the pedagogical conversations that would often occur while the copies were being made. Faculty began to come to the center less often, and we weren't able to talk with teachers about their writing assignments in the way we did before. In one staff meeting, we wanted to take time to think about the use of the word "help" on a writing center exit survey form: did we want to frame writing center work as "help" or as something else? This discussion, and other similar attempts to delve into praxis, was regarded as an attempt to needlessly complicate what was regarded as a simple practical matter.

In *Good Intentions: Writing Center Work for Postmodern Times*, Nancy Grimm argues that

> Theory often works [by] haunting and worrying us and only some-
> times instructing us in practical decisions. Because theory is powerful
> [and often remains half- or un-spoken], it often overtakes practices,
> alienates us from our intentions, silences what we know about what we
> do, and subjugates the daily knowledge that might challenge it. (ix)

But far from being "haunted" or "worried" by theory, or needing theory to counter prevalent misconceptions about writing center work, we found that we hungered more and more for theory to understand new practices that diverged from our expectations of writing center work.

We met often to discuss how changes in daily writing center operations represented theoretical shifts for the center and how we might use this knowledge to argue for alternatives to these changes, when warranted. Through these conversations, we came to understand that it was our mission as administrators to theorize more, not less, to be conscious of ways that the culture of the writing center was interacting with the people it meant to serve. We researched writing center scholarship in order to read the situations we were in and learned to describe our situation in both theoretical as well as concrete, personal terms.

In "The Idea of a Writing Center," North argues that "Writing centers [. . .] need time and space for appropriate research and reflection if they are to understand what they do, and figure out how to do it better" (445). Grimm concurs that writing center staffs need to create an adequate space to theorize about their mission and their practices:

> To legitimate themselves as academic units rather than as service units, writing centers need to undertake an ongoing effort to justify their practice theoretically rather than numerically. In order for writing centers to better clarify their function in higher education and improve their relationship with composition, they need to define their own priorities and beliefs in a context that exceeds yet respects the local context. Knowledge of how the system works, what the system expects, must be tempered by what writing centers learn about who students are. ("Rearticulating" 534–5)

As the interim director's insistence on the practical persisted, we learned to theorize more, if only for our own understanding of the disruptions between theory and practice. Through experience, we understood why Grimm insists that a writing center staff should cultivate a "relentless reflection" allowing the staff to see these disruptions and create "conditions for social transformation because it weakens the confidence derived from naturalizing the ways of the dominant group" (*Good Intentions* 109). This belief has brought us, in part, to write this chapter and to continue a reflective practice in our professional careers as a means to interrogate our practices, to act ethically in our work, and teach consultants to value reflective practice as a vital—and non-negotiable—part of writing center work.

The experience of finding ourselves in the front lines of a pitched battle to establish control and determine the future of our writing programs often felt—and was often represented by concerned others—as a "loss of innocence" because it had exposed us to the tangled and puzzling character of these struggles before we had even finished our dissertations and graduated. It would have been easy for us to turn cynical about writing center work or about academia, at least. But in fact, what we found is that through the experience, the fundamental writing center principles sustained our resolve. The effect of the losses we encountered was to reaffirm the validity of writing center work. Barbara Walvoord has written that "it is the *power* of a movement that [she] covet[s] for WAC" as it negotiates what she calls the "Darwinian" struggles among programs and movements on college campuses (291, 285). We felt that we were part of that struggle, arguing in ways available to us for an idea of a writing center that was quickly slipping. Boquet points out that it is important to speak up for the ideals we are working towards, even in moments of administrative crisis:

> Dislocation is a traumatic experience, involving separation and loss
> even as it holds the potential for relocation and regeneration. In times
> of such dislocation, noise should be expected and recognized for what
> it is: an attempt to alert others. To warn them. To gain assistance. To
> gather sympathy. To raise awareness. (6)

Boquet asks us to "consider the kinds of noise that we are asked to make, that we are allowed to make, that we are supposed to refrain from making, as we experience dislocations in our university communities and in our professional conversations" (6). As we negotiated our situation, we turned naturally to the practices that we value in writing centers: we conversed; we read; we theorized; and we wrote. Sometimes we did so privately, but often we chose to "make noise." As Blake reminds us, "without contraries, there is no progression" (50).

Works Cited

Blake, William. "From Songs of Innocence and of Experience: Shewing the Two Contrary States of the Human Soul." *The Norton Anthology of English Literature*. 3rd ed. Gen. Ed. M.H. Abrams. New York: Norton, 1975. 1306–1317.

_____. *Songs of Innocence and of Experience: The Illuminated Books*. Ed. Andrew Lincoln. Princeton, NJ: The William Blake Trust/ Princeton UP, 1991.

_____. "The Marriage of Heaven and Hell." Plate three. *The Norton Anthology of English Literature*. Vol. 2, 4th ed. Gen. Ed, M.H.Abrams. New York: Norton, 1979. 50.

Bloom, Harold, and David V. Erdman. "Notes on 'From Songs of Innocence and of Experience: Shewing the Two Contrary States of the Human Soul.'" *The Norton Anthology of English Literature*. 3rd ed. Gen. Ed. M.H. Abrams. New York: Norton, 1975. 1306–1317.

Boquet, Elizabeth H. *Noise from the Writing Center*. Logan, UT: Utah State UP, 2002.

Brereton, John C., Cinthia Gannett, Elizabeth Slomba, Katherine E. Tirabassi, and Amy Zenger. "'It Might Come in Handy': Composing A Writing Archive at the University of New Hampshire: A Collaboration between the Dimond Library and the Writing Across the Curriculum/Connors Writing Center, 2001–2003." *Centers for Learning: Libraries and Writing Centers in Collaboration*. Chicago: Association of College and Research Libraries Publications in Librarianship, 2005. 115–134.

"But Can They Write?" Editors. *Time Magazine/The Princeton Review*, Fall 2000: 63.

Glenn, Cheryl. *Unspoken: A Rhetoric of Silence*. Carbondale, IL: Southern Illinois UP, 2004.

Grimm, Nancy. *Good Intentions: Writing Center Work for Postmodern Times*. Portsmouth, NH: Heinemann, 1999.

_____. "Rearticulating the Work of the Writing Center." *College Composition and Communication* 47 (1996): 523–548.

IWCA Position Statement on Graduate Student Writing Center Administration. 2004. 13 January 2005. <http://writingcenters.org/gradpos.htm>.

Jackson, Rebecca, Carrie Leverenz, and Joe Law. "(Re)shaping the Profession: Graduate Courses in Writing Center Theory and Practice." *The Center Will Hold: Critical Perspectives on Writing Center Scholarship*. Ed. Michael Pemberton and Joyce Kinkead. Logan: Utah State UP, 2003. 130–150.

Leverenz, Carrie Shively. "Graduate Students in the Writing Center: Confronting the Cult of (Non)Expertise." *The Politics of Writing Centers*. Ed. Jane Nelson and Kathy Evertz. Portsmouth, NH: Boynton/Cook, 2001. 50–61.

North, Stephen M. "The Idea of a Writing Center." *College English* 46 (1984): 433–446.

Reynolds, Nedra. *Geographies of Writing: Inhabiting Places and Encountering Difference.* Carbondale, IL: Southern Illinois UP, 2004.

Rose, Shirley K. "Preserving Our Histories of Institutional Change: Enabling Research in the Writing Program Archives." *The Writing Program as Researcher: Inquiry in Action and Reflection.* Ed. Shirley K. Rose and Irwin Weiser. Portsmouth, NH: Heinemann-Boynton/Cook, 1999: 1074–118.

Simpson, Jeanne. "What Lies Ahead for Writing Centers: Position Statement on Professional Concerns." *Landmark Essays on Writing Centers.* Ed. Christina Murphy and Joe Law. Davis, CA: Hermagoras, 1995. 57–61.

Vaught-Alexander, Karen. "Situating Writing Centers and Writing Across the Curriculum Programs in the Academy: Creating Partnerships for Change with Organizational Development Theory." *Writing Centers and Writing Across the Curriculum Programs: Building Interdisciplinary Partnerships.* Ed. Robert W. Barnett and Jacob Blumner. Westport, CT: Greenwood P, 1999. 119–140.

Walvoord, Barbara. "The Future of WAC." *College English* 58 (1996): 58–79.

PART II

Between:
The Ways Graduate Students Challenge
Writing Center Theory and Practice

CHAPTER 6

A Writing Center in a Graduate School of Education:

Teachers as Tutors, and Still in the Middle

Helen Snively

Today, most writing centers have the goal of helping writers become better writers. And writing center scholarship abounds with suggestions, strategies and techniques for helping writing center tutors accomplish this worthy goal. However, until quite recently, much of the attention of this scholarship has been on undergraduate tutors and clients. For ten years, from 1994 to 2004, I developed and led a writing center entirely for graduate students, staffed mostly by doctoral students.[1] This rich experience provided me with insight into the ways writing centers can help even more experienced writers, like those pursuing master's and doctoral degrees, become better writers. Many of the clients who visited our center were working on papers for publication, dissertation proposals, and other in-depth research projects—projects that many typical undergraduate writers would not be engaged in. Still, our clients benefited from our writing center in many of the same ways that undergraduate writing center clients do.

Our center, the Writing, Research, and Teaching Center (WRTC) at the Harvard Graduate School of Education (GSE), developed out of a popular non-credit course called Graduate Writing, which had been offered for nearly 20 years. The course's sections, led by teaching assistants (TAs), were peer-response groups to which students brought drafts of papers they were writing for other courses. In 1994, the course's three TAs, of whom I was one, began offering office hours. As the program grew, we added TAs with specific skills in research methods as well as a range of workshops. By 2004, we

---

[1] For more on writing centers specifically for graduate students, please see Snively, Prentice and Freeman, 2006. Based on an informal survey in the spring of 2004, we estimated that at least ten graduate schools, including several law schools, had a writing center for their students, often staffed by one professional or a handful of doctoral students. That chapter also contains a longer description of the WRTC.

were annually serving about 200 of the school's 1,000 students in 700 sessions/500 hours.

To get at the nature of how working with the WRTC affected clients, in the fall of 2003, I interviewed[2] ten doctoral students who had worked steadily with one or more of the WRTC's TAs during the 2002–03 academic year. Most clients spent that year focusing on thesis proposals or qualifying papers. I knew all ten students quite well, having worked with all of them at least once. Most clients had come to the WRTC long before they began writing their proposals, making them regular visitors to our center. Mostly women, my participants generally reflected the diversity of the GSE student body in terms of age, ethnicity, academic field, and professional background; several were also tutors in the center. I also interviewed one TA who was not a client.

To get at the nature of the relationships these doctoral students developed with the TAs, I asked three basic questions: What kind of work did you do with faculty? What did you do with peers, either individually or in study groups? And how were these two types of relationships similar to or different from what you did in the WRTC? I expected that by thinking about their involvement in these three types of relationships, participants would highlight what was valuable about their work in our center.

Our conversations, averaging just under an hour, were comfortable and engaged. Participants occasionally touched on their work with me as well as that with the other TAs. To analyze the data gathered in the interviews, I transcribed my handwritten notes and used standard qualitative methods to find repeating themes, cluster them into categories, and create a narrative.

My analysis of our conversations suggests that clients viewed TAs in the WRTC in two ways. First, like peer tutors, we supported our colleagues' learning through conversation, and secondly, like writing teachers (but without the power to grade), we helped clients improve their writing. There are at least four overlapping aspects of our work, each exhibiting a different balance between tutoring and teaching. On the most basic level, the WRTC functioned like most writing centers; our tutors aimed to support students, served as sounding boards, clarified ideas, and decoded academic jargon. But our TAs were extremely skilled peers who had deeper and more varied knowledge about graduate level writing than most undergraduate tutors would probably have, and our TAs offered to share that knowledge. Third, some of our TAs were skilled in teaching through editing, and they were encouraged to offer that service. Finally, TAs sometimes functioned as surrogate faculty.

---

[2] To obtain informed consent, I gave each client a verbal explanation of my study and asked for their consent to participate. In addition, once I started analyzing my data, interviewees were given drafts of the chapter and had the opportunity to make any corrections to my representations of them or their words that they felt were inaccurate. In order to ensure anonymity, all names in this chapter are pseudonyms.

Tutor: The Core

I begin my description of our actual work, as many have, with Muriel Harris. Three elements of the tutoring relationship she describes seem especially applicable to work with graduate students: collaborative talk, affective support, and decoding academic jargon to assure students they are on the right track. First, Harris says that "writers both need and want discussion that engages them actively with their ideas," perhaps "[t]ossing around ideas to see how they play out" (31). One GSE doctoral student, Wanda, described a similar relationship with several TAs in the WRTC:

> The faculty always want a completed something, an end product. . . .
> To get from the idea to the end product is arduous. That's where the
> writing center serves me. I can talk randomly about where the parts fit
> together, and map [the structure of my literature review] on the white-
> board. (personal interview)

Wanda would come to the writing center with a few pages of text, looking for a "sounding board, an objective reader." Leila, Wanda's tutor, just let Wanda talk, challenging her when she did not understand. Perhaps most importantly, according to Wanda, "Leila listened." Wanda said this kind of active listening was something she could not get from faculty who "were not willing to brainstorm" with her. Terri, another doctoral student working with Leila, described her as a translator "between my notes and a structured product." Kitty, still another of Leila's clients, talked about Leila's "skill in clarifying/reframing in dialog."

Besides the TAs being sounding boards, clients talked about the importance of the affective support and reassurance they received from the TAs. Many clients were grateful to be in the one place in GSE where they sensed no "penalties for asking what they perceive[d] as 'dumb' questions" (Harris 28). Liz, a doctoral student, said it was okay to bring her proposal to the WRTC and "ask, '*Is* this a methods section?'" She was also glad to hear her draft was ready for faculty to read.

Tutors validated students' work in many other ways. Some clients simply sought confirmation that tutors understood what they were trying to say; Terri, for example, said it was valuable to find a TA who could step back and offer "new eyes. . . Am I communicating what I think I am?" And she found it very satisfying when, after a couple of sessions, her TA could say, "This is clear." The validation Wanda sought was about having something to say. She described working with another tutor, Michaela, who—valuably—did not know about Wanda's topic; therefore, Wanda and Michaela spent much time mapping her thinking. "The whole research process," Wanda said, "can make you so insecure. . . 'Do I have something to say?' And with [Michaela], I found I did."

For Kitty, the most important validation was about her own level of knowledge. Kitty and I worked together intensively on a long paper, and she remembered a turning point in her thinking when I asked her, genuinely curious, how much she actually knew about the work she was describing. She "suddenly spewed out information," and I was able to say "Oh, you do know!" For Kitty, "That was validating . . . my first 'I'm not alone here.'" Finally Liz, a TA and WRTC client, described how the center served her: we were an audience; we gave her a sense of the work itself, and we validated her work. "I'm emerging as an academic/writer/researcher, so these conversations are where I bring the evidence of my developing thoughts. It's important to be able to show the work."

In addition to being a place to share evidence of developing thoughts and a safe place to ask questions, the WRTC served as an emotional safe haven. One client, Catalina, spoke of the center as "a relief," as she would not have to "owe a favor" to the classmate who would read drafts for her. Another client, Jan, said she found safety in not having to rely on feedback from classmates whom she saw as "ultimately competitive." To Michaela, who was both a TA and client, the center became a "home," especially after Leila, an old friend, also began working there. These themes of support and validation reappeared frequently throughout my conversations with clients.

Third, Harris describes the writing center as a place to interpret the meaning of academic language, helping students "understand what to do with an assignment" (36). Much of our work, especially with EdM students, was decoding assignment sheets; we helped students to make sense of new genres and faculty expectations, and to see that yes, they were "on the right track" (39). We also encouraged students to come to us with their feedback from TAs and faculty across the school as well as their advisors and thesis committee members—and even the school-wide Committee on Degrees (COD) that evaluated the thesis proposal. We were often able to help clients see the supportive intentions in feedback that at first seemed negative or overwhelming. Though I do not have the data to claim that we kept anyone in school, students often said we made a critical difference when their proposal or other important paper had been criticized or even rejected.

Thus our tutors, like those in many writing centers, "inhabit[ed] a middle ground where their role [was] that of translator or interpreter, turning teacher language into student language" (Harris 37). Indeed, we spent much of our time in the "contact zone somewhere between teachers and students" (37). Graduate students need help with thinking and decoding as well as affective support just as much as undergraduates, and the ways we provided that support seem quite similar.

Highly Skilled Peer Tutor

According to Harris' description, then, our TAs were peer tutors, but their solid grounding in educational theories and the research process let them offer much more than just listening and clarifying. Students knew we often had enough domain knowledge to engage deeply in the conversation about a topic as a very informed audience. Catalina, a client, was grateful that we could suggest connections between ideas or even suggest sources to read. Other students appreciated being able to discuss a current theory as it applied to their work or they wanted help developing a strategic response when a proposal was rejected. Though tutors in every writing center will engage deeply in conversation with a peer, few undergraduates, or even beginning doctoral students, can also bring to that conversation a deep knowledge of both the field and the proposal-writing process. This may be one area where the WRTC was able to make a unique contribution—and the TAs thrived on being able to share their knowledge.

It was in the area of research methods, both qualitative and quantitative, that our TAs functioned as especially skilled peers, able to answer questions and make suggestions on many aspects of the research process. One of our TAs, Jesse, was known as "the methods maven." Another TA, Michaela, was known for her ability to provide quick answers to questions on statistics. Michaela also had "lots of knowledge you don't get in courses," according to Catalina, a student grateful that she could come to the TAs to check on such questions as "Do I need a chi square or a T-test?" And various TAs were known for having specific kinds of expertise on proposal writing, from the appropriate boilerplate for a particular paragraph, to what went in each section, to what might happen next in the process of proposal approval. Though, as Leila said, we would never "impose" our teaching, we all carried kit bags of various skills and areas of expertise.

Editor

In addition to teaching specific skills in our writing center, we also worked with students on improving their texts through editing. Linda Shamoon and Deborah Burns also argue for the value of editing. They describe Burns's advisor in a master's program who edited her thesis draft, not only providing appropriate formal vocabulary but even writing sentences that "helped locate" her work in her particular field. Though "it went against everything she had learned in composition studies," it made her "thesis and other academic writing. . . much less of a mystery" (229).

Developing their ideas on teaching through editing, Shamoon and Burns describe the classical musician's master classes, a practice they say is also accepted in many other fields: studios are standard practice in art and architecture programs, as are clinicals in nursing and grand rounds in medicine (231–233). In a master class in any field, the student watches how the master handles problems, and then internalizes that knowledge and skill, in a process that is "far more efficient and often less frustrating than expecting students to reinvent these established processes" (234).

Shamoon and Burns's account of master classes reminds me of Xiao Yan, my Chinese classmate who had been struggling to communicate his uncertainty over one finding in his thesis. Finally, his statistics professor gave him the wording he needed: "However, I remain open to the notion that . . . ." XiaoYan described the experience to me: "I started sighing. . . . OK, I felt the burden was gone. . . . This was very helpful" (Snively 90). Would he have found that wording himself? Brilliant as he is, I am reminded of the phrase about the monkeys at typewriters trying to write Shakespeare. For Xiao Yan, the professor's decision to provide that one line was efficient, ended his frustration, and let him turn to more productive work.

Multiple experiences with students like Xiao Yan showed me the value in direct rewriting and encouraged me to apply the technique in the WRTC, whether to rework a phrase or thoroughly edit a page or two. Our faculty director, Bruce McPherson, also modeled this work in his lectures and encouraged WRTC tutors to do it in office hours. For example, as I edited draft after reworked draft of Wanda's seven-page proposal, I asked her why I made each change. As she named the reason for each change, in comments like "Oh, yeah, better word," and "Right! I didn't need to explain that," she learned to sharpen her own writing. By semester's end, Wanda could edit for herself and brought me a draft I could scarcely improve. In a sense, I was giving a one-person master class, transmitting to Wanda what I had learned from Bruce. The TAs did the same for their clients, sharing what they had learned from Bruce, from me, and from each other.

Wanda was not alone. Students of all backgrounds asked us to cover their pages with red ink. Some, especially those from East Asia, told me they had learned English through their teachers' "corrections," and they expected the same from us. As I apologized to one student for using so much red ink, she said, "Helen, we crave correction!" Though the literature on second-language writing reflects considerable controversy over the efficacy of this approach (Qi & Lapkin 280), I endorse it, having watched it work for twenty years. Direct correction certainly works with adult students who are eager to improve their writing, especially if tutors extend to editing the common practice of insisting that students name and record what they learn. A professor of language acquisition at GSE also endorsed the practice, remarking in public on how much she learns as others edit her work. She also sent her international students to us, expecting we would give them the same treatment. Students saw direct correction as professional behavior. Catalina, a native speaker of Spanish, saw that "all good writers get editing—professional writers, published writers." As members of her research team edited her work, she always saw "the balance: are the ideas fuzzy or the words?" The correction process gave her both skills and confidence in her ideas.

I admit that our willingness to edit created some dilemmas. How to accommodate the international student who so craved learning through editing that she wanted every paper edited—no matter how time-consuming we found it? Or the older or more experienced student with a crucial document who expected perfect grammar and the exact turn of phrase from a foreign-born, or less experienced, TA? Though such instances of mismatch surely occur in every writing center, for us they seemed to arise most often around demands for editing, and sometimes around our intensive thesis-support services. Our response to these issues was to post brief bios of the TAs on our website so clients could choose a tutor whose background and skills seemed most appropriate. We also reminded students—repeatedly—that editing was far from our primary function.

We also struggled with the common issue in writing centers of how much proofreading to provide. During a year of campus-wide anxiety about plagiarism, we publicized a policy of no proofreading whatsoever. The WRTC was educational not editorial. Later, we learned we had alienated a significant group of our international students for whom proofreading likely meant copy-editing: if we were not willing to teach them fine points of English grammar, they asked, how could we possibly be any use to them? In time, we saw both the futility of trying to maintain the no-editing policy and the ethical issue involved in turning these students away when they clearly needed the training. We realized we could be both educational and editorial.

Shamoon and Burns also describe offering models to students, another approach we used in the WRTC, adopting it from general practice in the school. GSE faculty members frequently offered model papers for students to consult, as one more way to help them master unfamiliar genres. The WRTC had a file drawer of nearly fifty proposals that doctoral students could use as models, and we advertised this resource widely. Some students did adopt—and adapt—a line or two of boilerplate, saving them hours inventing their own, but we had little fear of anyone using more than that, as every study is so different. Moreover, students could absorb the proposal genre by analyzing how others had made a particular claim, connected two arguments or bodies of literature, responded to a "current conversation in the literature" (Shamoon and Burns 237) or made the rhetorical moves, for example, between statement of problem, research question, and methods. Though these skills are crucial for all doctoral students, we found that they may not always be transmitted in methods courses or by faculty advisors. Moreover, I discovered that students educated in Asia especially expected to learn from models, made efficient use of the drawer, and were eager to contribute their own proposals to the collection once they passed. Providing models is a small example of a culturally appropriate response to student needs. Thus, like Shamoon and Burns who stress teaching genre and the details of writing in a specific discipline, I believe models can be very effective when we are focused on transmitting skills to professionals who need to acquire a wide knowledge of genre.

Faculty Surrogate

Finally, at times, we unabashedly took on work that faculty could also do, helping students move through the process of proposing, conducting, and writing up their dissertation research. I find no mention in writing center literature of others doing such work as it lies so far out of the usual realm of writing center consulting and focuses more on the research process. But advising on the research process became a natural part of our work, especially after we integrated the Research TAs. Interestingly, even in this work we often remained non-directive peers.

In this work, we shared what we knew of the research process, starting with the less obvious but crucial tasks like developing a theoretical framework and shaping the research question that make it possible to develop the research methods and then write the proposal. On these tasks, and others, we could substitute for faculty, at least briefly, in addition to dipping into the kit bag of roles I described earlier, from sounding board to experienced peer who knew the ropes, to instructor in what makes good style in the genre. We did save faculty some time by helping students focus and polish their work before they went to meet them; saving faculty time was a specific goal when we first hired the research TAs. Such moments of faculty-like work also occurred as we ran thesis groups and mentored students through using the proposal drawer.

Students sought these services for good reason. Like faculty anywhere, those at GSE are extremely busy with research, publications, and travel. As a result, students told me, their advisors chose to engage in fairly specific activities—suggesting topics and readings, talking through theories and ideas—and then left students to write their proposals. The ten students I interviewed described how they wrote their drafts alone or with peers or study groups and with us, and then returned to faculty when they felt their draft was ready. Thus, even at this level of expertise, the WRTC was that place in the middle where clients could work on their drafts.

Chris, for example, knew his famous and very busy advisor would only discuss the big picture with him, never the details of his research project. But Chris accepted this— "We know the faculty are stretched thin, so we're content with what feedback we get," and Chris came to the WRTC to fill in the details. Likewise, though Kitty's busy advisor thought her ideas were interesting, he was "more big picture, very little concrete." He liked "to fine tune [at the end], not think it through from the start... not engage in narrowing down the topic." And Wanda said, "When I'd gotten what I could from my advisor, I needed to write and be sure I was understood. Leila was the translation between my notes and a structured product.... that work was the start of my real writing process."

Almost Like Faculty

These clients listed several specific activities their advisors would engage in; sifting through my interview data, I later discovered we had performed each of these tasks for at least one of them. First, some advisors, like Catalina's, would "hold the process... my thinking, my background, the history of my ideas. When I go to see him I don't need to explain it all again." Second, to help frame their research, faculty would commonly "talk about the big picture" and advise on research methods. Later, as faculty read fairly solid drafts, they would comment on content, point out inconsistencies and gaps in logic, and anticipate the reaction of the school-wide Committee on Degrees (COD). Finally, some faculty would edit or suggest ways to restructure.

On the first point, holding the process, I described above how, in working with Kitty, Leila would suggest what was coming next but still focus on working with her in the moment, remembering the current process. Similarly, Liz described how the WRTC could hold her process: "[the WRTC] gives me some static; it holds one part still," letting her work on the rest. Second, the research TAs constantly discussed the big picture and methods. For example, Jan, a student, described how Robin, a TA whom she saw as an expert in methods, helped her develop a new methodology for her research. In practice all of us helped students—and each other—to shape theoretical frameworks, research questions, and more.

Third, like their advisors, we could sometimes comment on content and always looked for gaps in logic. But the limits on our knowledge let us offer "new eyes," and thus serve as what Robin called "a surrogate audience," standing in for the COD. Two students clarified the difference between our position and that of faculty. First, Chris valued our "position as one step away" and was reassured when we could understand his work without being familiar with the literature ourselves. He saw us as "a barometer to measure clarity," a critical resource because the COD is also unfamiliar with any student's specific research topic. The look on my face as I read various parts of a draft was "very legitimate feedback" for Chris, a proxy for the way a professor or the COD would see it. Kendra made a different distinction between her work with faculty and with Robin, the tutor, based on the position their knowledge afforded. "They are both looking for gaps in my logic," she said, but from different perspectives. "So they're looking for different gaps." She found it useful to have Robin, as an "outsider" to her specific field, look at her work before she went to her faculty members, who were "insiders."

Fourth, like faculty, we were willing to edit and suggest restructuring. Kendra described how Robin would offer insights that might lead her to change her text or would sometimes suggest the changes directly, asking "What would happen if we tried this?" She said faculty members would do essentially the same thing. Neither, she said, was completely directive; the choice was always up to her. The difference was that Robin's insights would lead Kendra to make her own change whereas she might feel more obligated to accept suggestions from faculty members who would "have a stronger mental model and know the material." Here we see a client retaining ownership entirely in her work with a writing center TA, but gracefully accepting direction from a faculty member.

In many ways, then, the TAs in the WRTC served the same functions as faculty members. We engaged deeply with students, held their work as they moved through it, helped them shape their work, and sought clarity. We shared our expertise on methods, on writing, and on the overall process.

But Not Quite Like Faculty

On the other hand, WRTC clients were very clear on how we differed from faculty. Unlike faculty, we were not world-class experts on content—but that let us provide useful perspectives. And we did have time to help tease out the best way to word a key sentence. Perhaps most importantly, we were in no position to judge, though we were in a position to offer support and share the process. For most of these students, freedom from judgment was the clearest distinction between the WRTC and faculty. Michaela said, "At the WRTC I don't feel judged. I don't have to prove myself. It feels like home." Similarly, Catalina spoke of being anxious even in a close and trusting relationship with her advisor: "He's my mentor, but still you want polish. That judgment is suspended in here. I don't know if the judgment comes from the faculty or from myself, but you know it's part of the dynamic." Robin explained how he saw his role as tutor: "We're not the authority. We have the experience, the expertise, but not the power to approve or deny. So we're secondary, transitional." At the same time, students did expect us to be challenging, honest, and critical. One client said the first TA she went to was "too nice," so she sought out others. And Chris was grateful that "here, the reading is live, honest, critical, but not judged." Other clients were grateful that a TA could tolerate the messiness of qualitative research, expect many iterations, and accept a slow ongoing process without judging.

Time was also key for many clients. When I asked Kitty to compare her work with Leila and with her extremely busy advisor she said, "Oh, apples and oranges. . . . I got very little time or follow-up from him . . . just comments on paper, not engagement or what to do with the comments. . . . The faculty are time-limited, time is precious, and their judgments matter." In contrast, Leila could remember Kitty's work, and could engage, quickly, without judgment. Robin also saw us as having more time, "similar goals but more time for details." This time allowed involvement. Virtually all students I interviewed offered phrases like "involved in my process," "there for me," or "companion" in a long and lonely process. Miriam valued having "a relationship, not just one meeting," and Kendra found it helpful to work consistently with Robin, on different versions of her work.

Students pointed out differing aspects of this engagement. Three spoke gratefully of feeling entitled to the service with no need to return a favor to a peer. Several mentioned the accountability that comes with engagement. When Terri described her advisor as being accessible, I asked why she also came to Leila. Her answer: "For discipline and structure, and accountability." Similarly, Kitty remembered that back in her first year, facing the first paper she found truly difficult, I had been "someone to be responsible to—someone who's not an authority." Clients also appreciated continuity, the ability to return to someone who would remember their work and "sustain the dialog" with no need "to start over, to explain" the work again. That continuity could compensate for the short appointments.

These comments from students lead me to think that engagement remained the most important aspect of our work. Though they valued our expertise in many areas, what clients most appreciated was the attention, the memory, the teaching in the form of helping them figure out the steps. Though we clearly functioned as experts, as providers of key information, our most important role was probably being skilled listeners, in short, tutors.

So, whether we were tutors, teachers, editors, or almost faculty, we still occupied that "middle" space that Harris describes, the place where students work out details before returning to faculty. Chris said, "There's no direct link between my computer and the faculty. There's got to be a pit stop at the writing center, or a friend." Robin, a tutor, described his work as helping students "get their ducks in a row" before they took their latest revision of a proposal or thesis chapter to their advisor. Whether they saw themselves as competing in an auto race or a shooting gallery, virtually all these doctoral students agreed on the metaphors. Terri described how she would work out ideas with her advisor, then come to us, then back to the advisor, then to us, and then finally submit her work to the COD. Wanda said, "The faculty expect coherence. You need to be professional when going to them." Miriam said, "For 95% of the faculty, you can't go with messy stuff"; she saw it as a matter of "their time and your reputation." Finally, Jan and her study group had worked out which faculty members could and could not tolerate messiness and were strategic about coming to us before the high-stakes meetings with faculty.

Final Thoughts

For all of these doctoral students on the cusp of their dissertation research, we primarily served as the same kind of tutor Muriel Harris describes: that person in the middle who helps writers negotiate all of the complex tasks that they face. Though Harris describes working with undergraduates, I believe that our graduate student writers benefited in many of the same ways. In addition, they gained specific skills that, in other contexts, might be offered in courses. Thus I would argue that writing centers can be a vital component of writing education for all students. I want to offer two other reflections on our experience.

First, the themes of growth and community were important for all these students. As the writing center is for many undergraduate tutors, a graduate-focused center can also be a place of growth for its tutors. As Miriam, one of our less experienced tutors, developed a proposal, she met frequently with Robin and Liz, two of the most experienced. Not only did Miriam trust them to "know the ropes of qualitative" methods, she also developed her skills in writing, research, and tutoring through her work with them and shared those skills immediately with the clients who came to her office hours. Miriam was not alone in this learning process. Like any writing center, we made a point of sharing teaching techniques in our staff meetings; the tutors also signed up for office hours with each other and with me which allowed us all to share—and discuss—these skills. In time, for some tutors, the WRTC became a home, a place where colleagues were also friends and mentors. For example, Michaela was delighted at feeling entitled to have her friend Leila "there for me" in the hardest phases of working on her proposal.

And as Liz and I spoke about the WRTC as providing validation for students, she mentioned her own growth there: "For years, I've been a writer, teacher, and researcher into teaching. I came here to develop all those parts of myself. And I feel myself developing my identity as an author, an authority, as I show my work to others on the team, as I bring them the evidence of my developing thoughts." She continued, "This community is unique in GSE because we focus on how writing and research overlap. As I'm constantly talking about these connections in my work as a TA, I'm aware that my own skills as writer and researcher—and teacher of writing and research—are developing." Her point—that growth comes from the combination of sharing work and reading others'—is a common one in writing center work. For example, Shamoon and Burns describe the writing center as a place where a student can develop through practice using "domain-appropriate rhetoric" and expressing "new social identities" (238). My experience shows how such growth in community also occurred among the doctoral students who staffed the center. This kind of growth offers another rationale for having doctoral students engage in this sort of work with their doctoral peers: as doctoral students develop, they can enter the pipeline of faculty preparation I mentioned earlier.

Second, I hope our experience will allow others to develop more ways of working with graduate students. I believe this flexible combination of tutoring and direct teaching—doctoral students mentoring other doctoral students in the disciplines—will be crucial as faculty are increasingly stretched thin on nearly every campus. But this work need not always be done individually, as our course and sections and workshops showed. I see value in semester-long study groups, started by a writing center staff member who can provide support if the group falters on its own. Writing center staff can also offer workshops or work with various groups within the school; at GSE these included study groups, small doctoral-only courses, and the doctoral student association. Such practices allow the writing center to integrate itself into the life of the school, bringing it more credibility.

Finally, with credibility comes status. I suggest that our experience, along with that of other writing centers that serve graduate students, can help address this perennial issue. Our center met the varied needs of both master's and doctoral students. The WRTC was widely accepted and very popular, a place to honestly and directly teach the many skills that students need. We were emphatically not marginalized. Can the popularity of centers like ours help reverse the image of writing centers as marginal and remedial? I believe that it is possible and that, some day, centers like ours will be seen as mainstream.

Works Cited

Catalina. Personal interview. 23 September 2003.

Chris. Personal interview. 23 September 2003.

Harris, Muriel. "Talking in the Middle: Why Writers Need Writing Tutors. *College English* 17 (1995): 27–41.

Jan. Personal interview. September 2003.

Kendra. Personal interview. September 2003.

Kitty. Personal interview. September 2003.

Qi, Donald, and Sharon Lapkin. "Exploring the Role of Noticing in a Three-Stage Second Language Writing Task." *Journal of Second Language Writing* 10 (2001): 277–303.

Liz. Personal interview. September 2003.

Miriam. Personal interview. 24 September 2003.

Michaela. Personal interview. 26 September 2003.

Robin. Personal interview. September 2003.

Shamoon, Linda K., and Deborah H. Burns. "A Critique of Pure Tutoring." *The Allyn and Bacon Guide to Writing Center Theory and Practice*. Ed. Robert W. Barrett and Jacob S. Blumner. Boston: Allyn & Bacon, 2001. 225–241.

Snively, Helen, Cheryl Prentice, and Traci Freeman. "Writing Centers for Graduate Students." *The Writing Center Director's Resource*. Ed. Byron Stay and Christina Murphy. Mahwah, NJ: Erlbaum, 2006. 153–163.

Snively, Helen. "Coming to Terms with Cultural Difference: Chinese Graduate Students Writing Academic English." Diss. Harvard Graduate School of Education, 1999.

Terri. Personal interview. 25 September 2003.

Wanda. Personal interview. 22 September 2003.

CHAPTER 7

Training as Invention:
Topoi for Graduate Writing Consultants

Christopher LeCluyse and Sue Mendelsohn

The Rhetorical Situation from the Graduate Consultant's Perspective[1]

When we train graduate students to work in the writing center, it makes sense to apply the same pedagogical approaches that work so well in our consultations with student writers. Our commitment to collaborative learning and our preference for nondirective methods invite consultants to share ownership of the training process. However, we have learned in our consultant training at the University of Texas at Austin's Undergraduate Writing Center (UWC) that these two tenets of writing center pedagogy aren't always enough. Graduate students exist in a kind of professional limbo, negotiating a nexus of discourses and demands that complicates their training as rhetoricians and writing consultants. Many are simultaneously learning to be teachers, consultants, and scholars—roles that require overlapping but sometimes conflicting skills. And they are asked, in each role, to take on the persona and responsibilities of a confident professional at the same time that they have neither the institutional power nor the experience to fully do so. Training graduate consultants effectively, we realized, requires acknowledging and speaking to those competing demands and making a clear argument for why training matters.

Conceiving of training as an argument—a rhetorical act—places us on familiar ground. Alongside composition studies, rhetoric forms the foundation of writing center work. Rhetoric offers ways of understanding the possibilities for communication, entering a conversation, and engaging in action. In the case of training graduate writing consultants, rhetorical theory offers heuristics for assessing consultants' training needs and designing a training program that responds to those needs in a local context. We applied two

---

[1] This chapter is based on the rhetorical situation and institutional realities of the writing center at the University of Texas at Austin. Even though the arguments we make throughout this essay are based on our local situation, we believe that our experience of viewing training in a rhetorical way can benefit many other writing center administrators and consultants.

rhetorical concepts to guide our thinking about the transformation of the UWC training program: the concept of rhetorical situation to assess consultants' training needs and the concept of *topoi* to fill those needs. Both concepts motivate audience-focused approaches that accommodate change and ask us to take local circumstances into account.

As our discussion will make clear, however, administrators' and graduate consultants' perspectives on those local circumstances may differ. The administrator who designs training for graduate students without fully considering the disjunctures between their concerns and her own perceptions of them may develop a consultant training program that is wonderfully efficient but not necessarily effective. How, then, can a writing center administrator address the concerns of graduate staff and still meet the needs of the institution? To answer this question, we examine the concerns, interests, and pressures many of our graduate students bring to their writing center training. Two case studies then illustrate different approaches to training: the first looks at the evolution of training at the UWC from 1993 to 2001. During these years, the Center's training focused on meeting institutional needs. The second case study looks at the current UWC program, Training *Topoi*, a rhetorically based approach that acknowledges the position of its graduate audience.

In the writing consultation, consultants help writers become more savvy, self-sufficient rhetoricians, asking them to consider audience, the timeliness of their arguments (*kairos*), the warrants underlying their arguments, their own credibility (*ethos*), and so on. Administrators should consider these same rhetorical issues when designing a training program for graduate consultants:

- How would we describe graduate consultants as an audience?

- What are their interests and academic specialties?

- What conditions are they working under?

- What assumptions about their professional personae and writing do they bring to the job?

- What pressures do they face?

- What training practices do graduate students regard as credible?

Responding to these questions defines the unique rhetorical situation—to borrow Lloyd Bitzer's term—out of which graduate students, in particular, formulate themselves as writing consultants. Bitzer defines "rhetorical situation" as the circumstance out of which rhetoricians produce discourse:

> Let us regard rhetorical situation as a natural context of persons, events, objects, relations, and an exigence which strongly invites utterance; this invited utterance participates naturally in the situation, is in many instances necessary to the completion of situational activity, and

by means of its participation with situation obtains its meaning and its rhetorical character. (303)

This relation of utterance to participation and activity conceives of rhetoric as a form not merely of communication but of action (a productive way to think about our own work with student writers). Bitzer emphasizes that exigence applies only to a need that has the potential to be met through rhetoric and that one's audience is limited to those who have the possibility to function as agents of change (304–305). The ability to make that change happen is limited by constraints: "persons, events, objects, and relations which are parts of the situation because they have the power to constrain decision and action needed to modify exigence" (305).[2] Constraints help the rhetorician define common areas of understanding that speakers and audiences share.

Applying Bitzer's rhetorical model to the training of graduate writing consultants, encourages us to step back from the initial drive to decide the best training and structure single-handedly. The first crucial step must be to assess consultants' needs, which will inevitably vary depending on local circumstances. The content and structure of training realize their significance only to the extent that they emerge from the rhetorical situation that compels them. Defining that situation requires us to consider who and where graduate students are: the personal and professional demands being placed on them outside of the writing center, their institutional status, and their goals. By taking those factors into account, training can make explicit the ways in which writing center work can help graduate students advance personally and professionally.

The rhetorical situation of graduate students in the writing center is dependent on their situation within the larger context of the university. Graduate students are apprentices who must play the role of experts. Such expertise, however, is expressed in different and conflicting ways. Some graduate students' scholarly fields, especially those students in fields other than composition/rhetoric, may valorize long, lonely hours of individual thinking, while their teaching and writing center work more likely emphasize collaboration. While graduate students struggle to take on a role of authority in their fields, they must negotiate authority in the classroom and the writing center differently. And graduate students' often precarious institutional standing (low pay, few or no benefits, reliance on the decisions of advisors for advancement) can send graduate students the message that they embody none of these roles authentically.

The fact that, at our institution, writing center administrators and consultants share the same physical and institutional space, however, does not mean that they necessarily share the same understanding of rhetorical situa-

---

[2] Constraints also include special *topoi* of a discourse community, discussed below.

ation. Here, reading Bitzer by the letter can be misleading since, according to him, exigence, audience, and constraints define a situation independent of the rhetorical players involved. One would therefore assume that all parties who share in this context would proceed from the same vantage point. Such shared understanding rarely plays out in reality, however. Contrary to Bitzer's assertion that a rhetorical situation arises from "natural context," Richard E. Vatz points out that no significance is inherent or objectively situated outside the players involved. Contexts and exigencies do not determine meaning, Vatz argues, but rather meaning derives from people's perceptions of the rhetorical situation: "Fortunately or unfortunately meaning is not intrinsic in events, facts, people, or 'situations' nor are facts 'publicly observable'" (462–3). "No situation can have a nature independent of the perception of its interpreter or independent of the rhetoric with which he chooses to characterize it" (461). Thus, rhetorical situation becomes a locus of multiple perceptions, interlocking and overlapping, isolated and disjointed. Vatz's critique of Bitzer helps account for fissures among the varying perceptions of consultants' rhetorical situations held by writing center administrators, institutions, and the graduate students themselves. In response to these multivalent perceptions, graduate consultants must produce the rhetoric of consultants, teachers, and scholars.

Administrators likely see a different exigence for graduate consultants' work in the writing center than the graduate students themselves. For administrators, graduate consultants' exigency is related to the local situation; graduate students fill writers' needs for collaboration with experienced writers, and administrators, in turn, fill the consultants' need for professional development and initiation into a field of academic discourse and practice. Graduate writing consultants are typically expected to engage in the discourse of two interrelated areas: that of writing consulting itself and the professional discourse of writing center scholarship. Consultants engage in the latter when they are trained and help train their colleagues, produce conference papers, and—more broadly—see themselves as professionals in the writing center.

However, it may be difficult for our consultants to invest in administrators' notions of their exigency because the consultants are working from a different perception of the existing rhetorical constraints. For example, like most professionals, graduate students work in order to pay the bills. When we take into account that most support themselves (and sometimes their families) on part-time pay, the primary exigence for writing center work becomes clear. The short-term nature of the work for some of our consultants may further the perception that the writing center is nothing more than a stopping place where graduate students pay their dues before moving on to their "real" jobs. Moreover, graduate students are constrained by their authority vis-à-vis an audience of undergraduate writers during a professionally ambiguous time; graduate students are neither true peer collaborators nor faculty members with job stability and full institutional legitimacy, yet they often have substantial disciplinary expertise. They also may be new instructors learning to take on the authority of teacher and evaluator in the classroom at the same time that they are learning to be non-evaluative collaborators in the writing center.

Therefore, our graduate students may not necessarily see writing center work as professional development, and, indeed, most of the graduate consultants are not looking for careers in writing programs. Even though writing consulting offers academics a wealth of valuable experience, many graduate students at our institution regard teaching classes, attending conferences, and submitting articles for publication in their field of specialization as more relevant to their professional development. Institutional pressures can seem to confirm this perception. Graduate advisors' desire to help their students complete the degree sometimes sends the message that any work not directly related to the subject of their study is a distraction. The position of our writing center and its director within the university may also exacerbate consultants' perception that writing center work is a diversion from progress toward a tenure-track job. If the larger institution likewise considers the writing center a "mere" student service where non-tenured administrators and low-paid consultants help students "fix" their writing, why would graduate employees see the center as anything other than a place to put in one's time before being allowed to do work that really matters (also see Nicolas)? None of this is to say that graduate students do not see the value in writing consulting; they are, however, learning several new roles that can sometimes compete and conflict with writing center work. Thus to carry exigence for graduate consultants, our training should make the explicit argument that consulting is vital to professional development. Making that argument effectively requires an audience-based approach informed by the rhetorical situation in which graduate students find themselves.

CASE STUDY 1: *Training to Meet Institutional Needs*

The evolution of the consultant training program at the University of Texas at Austin's Undergraduate Writing Center offers case studies in both institution-based and audience-based responses to consultant training. The UWC was founded in 1993 as a branch of the University's Division of Rhetoric and Composition. In ten years, it went from handling 1000 consultations annually to handling over 10,000. Its initially small staff grew to some ninety consultants and administrators. The UWC is administered by a director who is a tenured faculty member in the Division, a coordinator who

---

[3] Undergraduate consultants currently make up twenty percent of the staff. Unlike graduate consultants, they must complete a writing center internship course before applying for a regular position.

is a staff person, and three graduate student assistant directors. While the Center serves undergraduate writers exclusively, the majority of its consultants are graduate students from departments across campus. The UWC automatically hires third-year English doctoral students who teach one course in the Division and work seven hours per week in the UWC.[3] The first semester that these instructors work in the UWC is also their first semester teaching composition, during which they take the graduate seminar "Supervised Teaching in English." Since UWC appointments allow graduate students to work enough hours (twenty hours per week) to qualify for benefits, if these students choose not to work in the Center, they forfeit their health insurance and about one-third of their monthly pay. The UWC also hires graduate students (both master's and doctoral candidates) from various other departments. While a few work twenty hours per week, most work about ten hours per week to supplement their teaching appointments in their departments or other university jobs and thus receive benefits.

As the UWC grew, the training program underwent moderate revision; however, by 2000, it became clear that a more significant change was needed: attendance at training functions was low, and an otherwise conscientious staff had become disengaged. During the 2001–2002 school year, the UWC completely reassessed its approach to training and began working from a new model. The early training program, carried out from the Center's inception in 1993 through 2001, relied heavily on regular staff meetings to train its consultants. In its early years, mandatory weekly one-hour staff meetings were times to "discuss policy and procedures, share information, and raise issues of common concern" (Bowen, Voss, and Kimball). Graduate consultants were encouraged to present information about the Center's resources at staff meetings. In practice, though, administrators typically defined training needs, chose topics, and presented training sessions. As the number of consultants grew and their hours overlapped less (the UWC went from being open twenty hours per week in 1993 to being open fifty-eight hours per week in 2001), whole-staff meetings became more unrealistic to schedule. Consequently, the number of staff meetings decreased until 2001 when administrators required consultants to attend just two of three scheduled staff meetings each semester. Administrators had fewer meetings in which to address more business matters, sometimes struggling to squeeze training into the last 15 or 20 minutes of the session.

To make up for the decrease in training provided at staff meetings, administrators packed more training into the beginning of the semester before the first wave of student writers rolled in. While the training program in its initial year was "necessarily somewhat ad hoc" (Bowen, Voss, and Kimball 26), in subsequent years, administrators scheduled more formal training activities for the first two weeks of the fall semester to supplement staff meetings, instituting a fall orientation, consultant observations, and practice consultations in 1994 and adding training workshops in 1995 (26). In its early years, the fall orientation was a brief meeting that served as "a general introduction to the UWC and its administrative staff," focusing on administrative issues instead of pedagogical concerns (Bowen, Voss, and Kimball 8). By the end of the 1990s, however, one of the primary goals of fall orientation was to introduce consultants to writing center pedagogy and practice. The orientation became a four-hour affair held before the semester started, with new consultants attending the full session and returning staff attending the second half. Consultants were expected to come prepared to discuss several pre-assigned scholarly articles on writing center pedagogy. Administrators led the staff in discussing the articles, the Center's consulting philosophy, and—with the help of video clips of consultations—common consulting concerns and strategies.

Alongside the orientation, the first two weeks of training featured practice consultations, observations, and, later, workshops. During these two weeks, consultants were responsible for bringing their own writing to be consulted on and observing several consultations. In their first year, the workshops focused mainly on administrative and technology concerns; workshops were designed to "allow staff to practice consulting, learn the registration program [the Center's record-keeping system], and become familiar with the UWC's computers and software" (Bowen, Voss, and Kimball 11). By 1997, the workshops' focus shifted to consulting concerns; topics included "working with students on E306 [Rhetoric and Composition] assignments, talking to students about grammar, working with ESL students, and understanding writing practices in other disciplines" (Bowen, Voss, and Kimball 9).

In many ways, the UWC's pre-2002 training programs responded well to the needs of the Center. The early emphasis on learning administrative procedures reflected the organization's need to establish its role on campus with accurate record-keeping, efficient use of technology, clear policies for working with students and maintaining their confidentiality, and productive connections to academic departments and administrative units. Training at this time tended to be hierarchical as administrators worked to set the norms for the Center's operation. As those activities started to seem more like standard procedure, the UWC then turned to the issue of how to help its consultants work with the rapidly increasing number of writers who walked through the door. Compounding the urgency for training in pedagogical issues was the change in the kinds of writing students wanted to work on in the Center. In its first year, over 70% of clients were from the same composition course, Rhetoric and Composition, that most of the UWC consultants were currently teaching ("The UWC" 1). Thus, the consulting staff was quite familiar with the assignments most students were bringing in, and the consultants had a sense of common concerns those assignments raised. Just three years later, the percentage of Rhetoric and Composition students had dropped to 25 ("The UWC" 1). Moreover, as demand for consultations increased, so did the demand for consultants, and the coordinator began to hire more graduate students from outside the English Department—students who were not teaching composition and rhetoric but brought their own disciplinary expertise. The focus in training necessarily shifted to issues of pedagogy and practice as more and more students brought in unfamiliar assignments and often unfamiliar concerns. The training program had undergone considerable changes in its first eight years, but in response to what?

Taken as a whole, the evolution of graduate consultant training at the UWC from 1993 to 2001 shows a reduced emphasis on training for administrative concerns and an increase in training for pedagogical issues. This shift took place in response to changes in the Writing Center's audience and constraints: changes in the diversity of clients' concerns, growth in the numbers of clients served and consultants employed, increases in hours of operation, and the solidification of institutional policies and practices. These changes produced an exigence for rhetorical action; administrators developed training in response to what they saw as the Center's rhetorical situation.

Graduate consultants' rhetorical situations, however, had not been a major motivator of training decisions before 2001. And although the shift to more pedagogically-focused staff education had the potential to speak to graduate consultants' professional development needs, they still weren't engaged. The model of mixing training sessions with regular business meetings may have perpetuated the notion that writing center work is service work rather than an integral part of one's professional development. Contrary to Muriel Harris's suggestion that ongoing training take place during regular staff meetings, separating the administrative business of writing center work from pedagogy and practice helps us think of ourselves as professionals in a larger field rather than just employees in a specific office with its own unique practices. The trend toward front-loading more training into the beginning of the semester unwittingly sent the message that writing consulting is like riding a bicycle, a skill acquired once and quickly mastered rather than a discipline one must engage with continually. The Center failed to make a clear argument for the value of writing center work as professional development—to an audience who did not assume that they would find it there. Training topics were largely determined by administrators, and consultants, seeing their work as a task rather than a discipline, were content to let administrators lead training sessions. Training, then, was information to be received rather than a pedagogical discussion that consultants could actively shape. The unintended implication of this model was that administrators were the sole knowledge-makers and initiators, consultants passive and deficient in their knowledge. Therefore, although the training program evolved to meet the institution's needs, it confirmed consultants' belief that writing consultation had little to do with building professional expertise. The Center's administrators eventually recognized the shortcomings of a training system that responded to its own institutional needs well but did *not* take into account the concerns and needs of a largely graduate staff.

CASE STUDY 2: *Training to Meet Consultant Needs*

Addressing these shortcomings provided the UWC with a way to make training reflect the collaborative ethos of writing consultation and draw on the interests and expertise of its staff. Starting in the spring of 2002, the Center began offering Training *Topoi* (singular *topos*), weekly workshops on a variety of topics relevant to writing consultation, from fine points of grammar to careers outside the writing center. As we will explain in greater detail, the classical rhetorical term used to designate these training sessions indicates the dynamic role they play both in situating consultants in the standard discourse of writing center practice and in empowering consultants to reflect on those practices and invent new ones. This dual focus on the established and the new speaks especially to graduate consultants' rhetorical situations by acknowledging the various demands they face and by facilitating their transition from student to educator and scholar.

Training *Topoi* were originally coordinated by one of the authors, Sue Mendelsohn, then a graduate student assistant director. When it became apparent that scheduling, conducting, and videotaping *Topoi* was a job in and of itself, however, the UWC created a post-doctoral Training Specialist position (now filled by the other author, Christopher LeCluyse) dedicated to these and other training-related tasks. The Training Specialist, in consultation with the rest of the administrative staff, determines the themes of roughly half of the *Topoi*. Graduate and undergraduate consultants suggest topics for the other half and frequently present them as well. Most weeks in the UWC's training schedule feature at least one hour-long *Topos*—sometimes two or three. Attending three hours of *Topoi* fulfills consultants' training requirement for the semester, and staff are free to choose those *Topoi* that suit their interests and schedules.

Training *Topoi* can be divided into six broad categories according to focus: (1) writing consultation practice; (2) grammar and English as a second language; (3) the curriculum of the university's Rhetoric and Composition program, a significant source of UWC clients; (4) understanding the conventions of writing across the curriculum; (5) helping writers with materials, particularly personal statements, for professional and academic applications; and (6) consultants' own professional development. *Topoi* in the first category help the UWC both reinforce and constructively question the received truths of writing center praxis. For example, while the first semester of the training program featured "Break Out of Your Directive Funk," offering participants ways to keep consultations dialogic and student-focused, this past semester featured "Improvising in Consultation: When It's Okay to Be Directive," which invited consultants to discuss situations in which they felt that directly explaining what the writer should do was the most effective solution. *Topoi* on professional development have included a guest presentation by Joan Mullin on pursuing a career in writing center administration, as well as workshops by former UWC coordinator Elisabeth Piedmont-Martin and former consultant Michael Erard on writing and consulting outside an academic setting. Directors from other writing centers have also presented *Topoi* on how their centers are organized, administrated, and conducted; such presentations connect the UWC to writing centers at neighboring colleges and universities and expose our staff to institutional situations quite different from our own.

Drawing knowledge from staff as well as experts from outside the writing center emphasizes the collaborative nature of the work we do and breaks down the potential hierarchy between trainers and trainees. Each semester, the Training Specialist invites faculty, graduate students, and staff from other university departments to lead workshops. Recent *Topoi* have included a presentation on African American English by Lisa Green, professor of linguistics, and one on working with international students and alleviating writing anxiety from Leonór Diaz, a counselor at the university's Counseling and Mental Health Center. Graduate consultants have complemented these offerings by organizing workshops in their own areas of expertise. Susan Briante, a writer and PhD candidate in English, for instance, led a *Topos* on using creative writing strategies in consultation. Empowering graduate consultants to train their peers demonstrates that they, like administrators and outside authorities, are sources of expert knowledge (though, as will be seen, not the only ones). Drawing from this multiplicity of perspectives also brings Vatz's revision of Bitzer to bear on the training process. While graduate consultants can develop their consulting practice by considering others' perceptions of relevant *topoi,* they can also lend their own perspectives. After all, the only people who can fully and accurately define graduate students' rhetorical situations are the students themselves.

The way that *Topoi* are conducted also ideally reflects the center's collaborative culture. Although some topics lend themselves to a lecture format, the most successful and satisfying *Topoi* involve people sharing their experiences of and strategies for writing consultation. The Training Specialist encourages presenters to provide opportunities to discuss and apply the material being covered. As a result, consultants receive training not only from the presenter but from each other. The presenter of the *Topos* thus becomes more of a facilitator than the sole fount of knowledge, and consultants themselves realize the wealth of experience that they can share with their colleagues.

This focus on collaboration, process, non-hierarchical relationships, and fostering independence brings the values of writing center practice to bear on the consultants themselves—a consistency missing from the UWC's earlier training model. In its training, the Center now acknowledges that "what we experience as reflective thought is related causally to social conversation (we learn from one another)" (Bruffee 398). In this case, that reflective thought applies not only to writing but to writing consultation, an even more overtly social activity (cf. Trimbur 98–101). As consultation specialists operating both inside and outside writing centers continually reaffirm, such collaboratively fueled reflection is crucial for effective practice (see, for example, Lunsford 49; Schon 22–40).

The collaborative nature of Training *Topoi* make them most beneficial for consultants who can participate in person. However, the number of consultants that the UWC employs and their varied schedules mean that many cannot attend a particular *Topos*. Electronic media increases the "shelf life" of these training offerings by reaching consultants after the fact. *Topoi* are recorded on digital video and made available through a special section of the Writing Center's web site currently available only to staff. At the end of the semester, consultants who have not fulfilled their training requirement may watch these videos for credit but only after they have exhausted opportunities to attend in person.

Topoi Then and Now

As their name indicates, Training *Topoi* draw on a modern understanding of an ancient rhetorical concept. *Topoi* as described in Aristotle's *Rhetoric* are literally "places" in which rhetorical invention takes place.[4] Aristotle distinguishes general *topoi*—various ways of generating arguments such as by focusing on definition or correlation—from special *topoi*—themes particular to a discipline or domain. As Carolyn R. Miller explains, special *topoi* arise from "conventional expectations in rhetorical situations [note her use of Bitzer's term], knowledge and issues available in the institutions and organizations in which those situations occur, and concepts available in specific networks of knowledge (or disciplines)" ("Aristotle's 'Special Topics'" 67). Thus for the "specific network of knowledge" formed by writing centers, we can define such special *topoi* as respecting students' ownership of and investment in their written work, being nondirective and non-evaluative, and helping writers through a dialogic process.

Since *topoi* are both defined by the communities in which they circulate and provide points of departure for new arguments, they are at once predetermined and dynamic. Several rhetoricians have named this dichotomy in various ways. According to Richard McKeon, "The commonplace of commonplaces [his translation of *topoi*] is the place in which the certainties of the

---

[4] Equating an abstract endeavor, like generating arguments, with concrete locations is not without its dangers. As Richard McKeon observes, terms such as *topos* "were as ambiguous in ordinary Greek as they are in ordinary English, and the nature of 'place' and 'space' was a subject of dispute in the beginnings of Greek physical science" (25). Like many scholars of topical invention, however, we find this ambiguity to be productive: the notion of *topos* is itself a productive *topos*.

familiar are brought into contact with the transformations of innovation" (35). Drawing on this idea, Miller points out "a paradox: that *topoi* serve *both* managerial and generative functions—they can effect both novelty and decorum" ("The Aristotelian *Topos*" 132). Likewise, former UWC director Rosa Eberly describes *topoi* "as both source and limitation for further discussion and deliberation" (5). Recognizing both aspects of the *topoi* generated within a community maintains their dynamic nature.[5] In our particular case, treating the fundamentals of writing consultation not only as guidelines but also as sources of new practice keeps them from petrifying—an outcome to be avoided in a community that values the *topoi* of dialogue and process.

Although more concrete than their classical forebears, Training *Topoi* likewise emerge from the rhetorical situations of a community—in this case, those of both writing center administrators (three of whom are graduate students themselves) and the students who staff the center. The training model accommodates these varying perspectives by inviting *Topos* suggestions from both administrators and consultants and basing about half of the workshops on consultant-suggested themes. Here, again, Vatz is relevant: consultants' suggestions provide an inside look at their rhetorical situation that in turn helps administrators assess their training needs. Defining staff training in this way accounts for both the pre-existing constraints on writing center work—the shared knowledge, assumptions, and *foci* of the writing center community—and the novel perspectives that consultants bring to the center. Training *Topoi* on writing consultation practice, for instance, draw on such fundamental concerns as "Encouraging Without Evaluating" and "Keeping Writers Engaged." *Topoi* on grammar and English as a second language both derive from common approaches to language-level issues in writing center practice and composition studies and also respond to anxieties consultants frequently voice about identifying and explaining linguistic problems. Graduate students' interests in finding employment and developing professionally inform *Topoi* such as "Teaching/Consulting Symbiosis," on how consultation methods can influence teaching practice, and "Writing Consulting in the Real World."

Whereas these predefined concerns set the agenda for various Training *Topoi*, presenters' individual approaches and participants' discussion and responses complement the familiar with the innovative, to use McKeon's terms. A presenter may choose to expand upon or even resist the standard "takes" of writing center practice. Consultants, for their part, may brainstorm

---

[5] Failure to do so led to the devaluation of Aristotle's topical system. As McKeon relates, "Quintilian complained that many orators made collections of sayings and arguments concerning subjects likely to recur in the practice of their art instead of fortifying themselves with places by which to discover new arguments that had never occurred to them before" (28). Walter Jost and Michael J. Hyde echo Quintilian's concerns: "When topics ... get too uniformly or finely determined in their meanings, ... they cease to function as rhetorical places and become something, namely mere facts, or principles of a determinate inquiry, or ideology" (14).

new strategies or question the effectiveness of existing ones. Creating a space in which such innovation is sanctioned and encouraged imbues Training *Topoi* with the generative power of *topoi* in general.

Continuing Challenges in Implementing Training *Topoi* for Graduate Consultants

So far we have presented the Training *Topoi* model in idealized terms, passing over the inherent challenges of implementing such a system. The day-to-day reality of training graduate consultants in this way is, of course, more complex. Not all *Topoi* conform to a collaborative ideal; some presentations assume a traditional lecture format, a situation that at times encourages graduate consultants to revert to their familiar student roles. In short order, a room full of competent and knowledgeable people can become passive and silent, exchanging the role of expert for that of novice. Leaving attendance up to choice also means that even the best-prepared *Topoi* may attract only a few consultants.

While recognizing the particular rhetorical situations of both administrators and graduate students helps training evolve with the special *topoi* of the writing center community, larger institutional constraints are beyond our control. Since, as we have detailed, the UWC instituted Training *Topoi* in response to our own center's needs, the model may not be appropriate for centers with smaller staffs or different organizational structures. We believe, however, that writing centers of any size can still benefit from applying prevalent theories of rhetoric, composition, and writing consultation practice to how they treat and instruct their own staffs, especially when those staffs include graduate consultants who stand to benefit that much more from such treatment. Walter Jost and Michael J. Hyde affirm the value of such an approach:

> Rhetoric brings us back to a language of agents and agencies in which questions about who we are become repeatedly reworked in the places where we work. Topics [or *topoi*] provide an orientation and an ability to handle both settled social identifications and possible novel perspectives and values and in that way resist self-complacency .... (17)

Under the pressing demands of funding, institutional politics, and clientele, however, writing center workers can too easily distribute a humane and dynamic method of learning without receiving it themselves.

A happier challenge arises from acknowledging the mastery that consultants have already achieved. Experienced consultants may question the need for continued training on the grounds that they already have acquired a solid foundation in writing consultation. The independence they have gained as practitioners may in turn seem to obviate the need to exchange knowledge with others. Here again, the approach we take with student writers can recast the way we train staff. Just as writing consultants (as the name indicates) deal with writers "on the level," regarding consultation not as a remedy for those who lack skills but as a professional dialogue from which any writer can benefit, so administrators can approach training as a mutually beneficial dialogue among peers. Veteran consultants attend continuing training not because they lack knowledge but because they contribute to the knowledge of others—and continue to benefit from reflecting on their practices. If the notion of deficiency is inherent in training, then perhaps we need to employ a different *topos* in order to best facilitate graduate students' transition into mastery as scholars, teachers, and consultants.

Works Cited

Bitzer, Lloyd F. "The Rhetorical Situation." *Philosophy and Rhetoric* 1.1 (1968): 1–14. Rpt. in *Rhetoric: Concepts, Definitions, Boundaries.* Ed. William A. Covino and David A. Jolliffe. Boston: Allyn and Bacon, 1995. 300–310.

Bowen, Scarlett, Randi Voss, and Sara Kimball. *Undergraduate Writing Center Staff Handbook, 1993-1994.* Austin, TX: Undergraduate Writing Center, 1993.

Bowen, Scarlett, et al. *Undergraduate Writing Center Staff Handbook, 1994–1995.* Austin, TX: UWC, 1994.

_____. *Undergraduate Writing Center Handbook, 1995.* Austin, TX: UWC, 1995.

_____. *Undergraduate Writing Center Handbook, 1996–1997.* Austin, TX: UWC, 1996.

Bruffee, Kenneth A. "Collaborative Learning and the 'Conversation of Mankind.'" *College English* 46.7 (November 1984): 635–52. Rpt. in *Cross-Talk in Comp Theory: A Reader.* Ed. Victor Villanueva, Jr. Urbana: NCTE, 1997. 393–414.

Eberly, Rosa. *Citizen Critics: Literary Public Spheres.* Urbana, IL: U of Illinois P, 2000.

Harris, Muriel. "Selecting and Training Undergraduate and Graduate Staffs in a Writing Lab." *Administrative Problem Solving for Writing Programs and Writing Centers.* Ed. Linda Myer Breslin. Urbana, IL: National Council of Teachers of English, 1999. 14–29.

Jost, Walter, and Michael J. Hyde. "Rhetoric and Hermeneutics: Places Along the Way." *Rhetoric and Hermeneutics in Our Time: A Reader.* Ed. Walter Jost and Michael Hyde. New Haven: Yale UP, 1997. 1–42.

Lunsford, Andrea. "Collaboration, Control, and the Idea of a Writing Center." *The Writing Center Journal* 12.1 (1991): 3–10. Rpt. in *The St. Martin Sourcebook for Writing Tutors.* 2nd ed. Ed. Christina Murphy and Steve Sherwood. New York: St. Martin's, 2003. 46–53.

McKeon, Richard. "Creativity and the Commonplace." *Philosophy and Rhetoric* 6 (1973): 199–210. Rpt. in *Rhetoric: Essays on Invention and Discovery.* Ed. Mark Backman. Woodbridge, CT: Ox Box Press, 25–6.

Miller, Carolyn R. "The Aristotelian *Topos*: Hunting for Novelty." *Rereading Aristotle's Rhetoric.* Ed. Alan G. Gross and Arthur E. Wallzer. Carbondale: Southern Illinois UP, 2000. 130–146.

_____. "Aristotle's 'Special Topics' in Rhetorical Practice and Pedagogy." *Rhetoric Society Quarterly* 17.1 (1987): 61–70.

Nicolas, Melissa. "Writing Center as Training Wheels: What Message are We Sending our Graduate Students?" *Praxis* 3.1 (2005). <http://lovecraft.cwrl.utexas.edu/praxis>

Schon, Donald A. *Educating the Reflective Practitioner.* 1st ed. San Francisco: Jossey-Bass, 1987.

Trimbur, John. "Collaborative Learning and Teaching Writing." *Perspectives on Research and Scholarship in Composition.* Ed. Ben W. McClelland and Timothy R. Donovan. New York: MLA, 1985. 87–109.

Vatz, Richard E. "The Myth of the Rhetorical Situation." *Philosophy and Rhetoric* 6 (1972): 154–61. Rpt. in *Rhetoric: Concepts, Definitions, Boundaries.* Ed. William A. Covino and David A. Jolliffe. Boston: Allyn and Bacon, 1995. 461–467.

"The UWC: Three Years Later." *Writer's Block* 21 Nov. 1996: 1.

Chapter 8

Collusion and Collaboration:
Concealing Authority in the Writing Center

Brooke Rollins, Trixie G. Smith, and Evelyn Westbrook

On the first day of training at the University of South Carolina writing center, staff members, all graduate student assistants, receive a copy of the Philosophy and Mission Statement.[1] This required reading is intended to introduce them to the writing center's model of peer collaboration—a carefully crafted egalitarian code that emphasizes writing center assistants' duty to foster active learning and respect the expertise of their clients, whether freshmen or faculty. The Philosophy envisions the writing center as "a place for collaboration, one where any writer can come to think and talk about writing," and this investment in collaborative learning is meant, above all, to empower clients, to help them gain "confidence in their own abilities." Just as the Philosophy's emphasis on client empowerment guides how graduate students are meant to manage their sessions throughout the year, it also dictates how they should speak of themselves: "Since we value the positive effect collaboration has on writing and respect the background and expertise of our clients, those who work with clients are called 'writing assistants,'" rather than tutors or consultants, which both "imply a hierarchy."

Like those of many writing centers dedicated to developing better writers, the USC writing center Philosophy sets up a model of nonhierarchical, peer collaboration. The goals of this model are of course laudable, but even the most carefully modulated language devoted to collaborative learning in the writing center hints towards its tensions. According to the USC Mission Statement, the writing center staff "advises and mentors" clients and educators, and "fosters outreach programs." The Philosophy similarly determines that the staff "provide detailed, descriptive narratives about the session to teachers," "help clients" and "help produce better writers." These action verbs grant agency to graduate student assistants and imply that the staff has knowledge and power useful to writing center

---

[1] See Appendix One for a complete version of the Philosophy and the Mission Statement at the time of this study. We have chosen these two documents because 1) they are familiar to us and 2) they are representative of the well thought out documents that govern many writing centers.

clients. The assistants "advise," "mentor," and "help" others because they have more expertise, at least about writing. This expertise is emphasized when the writing center assistant is a graduate student in the English department. Not only do these writing center assistants have a better familiarity with the requirements and constraints of academic writing, but often times they also teach classes in the English department. Maintaining the roles of writing center assistant and writing teacher is a difficult proposition. In most cases, writing center assistants are not able to talk with clients about their writing in the same way they talk with their own students. They cannot know for sure the objectives of the writing assignment, and they are not supposed to say with authority how best the students should meet those objectives. For writing center assistants, the first priority is that clients think and talk about these objectives and find their own ways of meeting them. Even if they work exclusively in the writing center, the assistants' alignment with and allegiance to the institution compromises their "peerness." And yet the authority that graduate students in the writing center must manage is not clearly defined. Though they come to the writing center session more familiar with the rhetorical demands of academic writing, graduate students must also navigate their liminal position in the university. Located somewhere between undergraduates and faculty members, graduate students can simply occupy neither the role of peer nor the role of final authority over a client's writing project.

Clients, of course, also have their duties, but their duties—to "change" their perspective about the writing process, and "talk about and improve [their] writing"—imply that clients are somehow wanting, certainly not equal in expertise or authority to the graduate students who comprise the writing center staff. Like their assistants, clients must assume a delicate position. They are asked to participate in collaboration, even as they are reminded that they need the help of the writing center and its agents to change their view of the writing process and thus improve their writing.[2]

Writing center theory likewise points to the tensions inherent in peer tutoring and collaboration; though democratic ideals constitute its foundation, disparate power relations often gird its load-bearing wall. Andrea Lunsford advocates the collaborative writing center not only because "collaboration is the norm in most professions," but also because students in her classes reported that "their work in groups, their *collaboration*, was the most important and helpful part of their school experience" (emphasis in original 110–111). Lunsford's data furthermore suggest that collaboration promotes excellence by cultivating problem solving skills, sharpening critical thinking abilities, and encouraging active learning. And yet she insists that we use collaboration

---

[2] We are not being disparaging of the work at USC; rather we respect the valuable help the various writing centers offer students and faculty and wish to strengthen their services through an honest look at how these documents may be perceived.

cautiously in writing center practice "because creating a collaborative environment and truly collaborative tasks is damnably difficult" (111). More recent theory in our field seems to share Lunsford's caution, as it speaks more directly to the power relations inherent in the collaborative writing center. Irene Clark, for example, suggests that writing center theory and training should attend to the role of tutors' "directiveness," while Julie A. Bokser makes room for power differentiation among conference participants noting that the "egalitarian pose of peerness" (21) can cover over "the highly aggressive relationship between tutor and student" (21). When used to describe the dynamics of the writing center then, the word "collaboration" often masks the authority inherent in the writing assistant's role, especially when the assistant is a graduate student from the department of English.

Rather than striving to equalize asymmetrical power relations between clients and assistants, some writing center theorists insist on their pedagogical merit. Linda K. Shamoon and Deborah H. Burns, for example, argue that "directive tutoring . . . is sometimes a suitable and effective mode of instruction" (134). And in their 1998 linguistic analysis, Susan R. Blau, John Hall, and Tracy Strauss conclude that writing center assistants' use of questions, echoing, and qualifiers often wastes time in the attempt to create a collaborative-*sounding* environment. The authors argue that rather than making collaboration the main goal of each session, tutors should be judicious and flexible. "This is not to suggest that collaboration should be discarded as a goal of tutorial relationships. But collaboration, like any other teaching/learning mode, has to be used judiciously and appropriately" (38).

Because graduate students in the writing center maintain a highly complex role that requires them to draw upon their writing expertise while allowing clients to maintain ownership of their texts and participate actively in the tutorial session, striking the appropriate note of judiciousness and flexibility is no easy task. In an attempt to study how they go about balancing these demands, this project uses detailed transcript analyses of three writing center sessions conducted by graduate students at the University of South Carolina. Data from this linguistic study suggest that even as writing center assistants strive to create a collaborative environment, they struggle with their competing desires to appear nonauthoritative and to insist on their expertise.

Because we are interested in how writing center assistants deal with the demands to be at once experts on writing and collaborative "peers," the idea of collusion as it is articulated by R.P. McDermott and Henry Tylbor helps us to understand the complicated relationships between writing centers, graduate student writing center assistants, and their clients.

> Collusion refers to how members of any social order must constantly help each other to posit a particular state of affairs, even when such a state would be in no way at hand without everyone so proceeding. Participation in social scenes requires that members play into each other's

> hands, pushing and pulling each other toward a strong sense of what is
> probable or possible, for a sense of what can be hoped for and/or ob-
> scured. (219)

McDermott and Tylbor thus explain how participants in conversations work
together to construct social structures, roles, and relationships, and they consider both the positive and negative implications of such a construction. People collude in order to express their most optimistic hopes of what the world
should be even as they collude to perpetuate a "well-orchestrated lie that offers a world conversationalists do not have to produce but can pretend to
live by, a world everyone knows to be, at the same time, unrealizable, but
momentarily useful as stated" (220).

Because the writing center session is fraught with demands of both assistants and clients—demands they often meet but rarely talk about—we find
McDermott and Tylbor's idea of collusion particularly useful in our examination of writing center conversation. The sessions we examine in this study
suggest that the warning sounded by Lunsford still rings true. She writes
that "collaboration often masquerades as democracy when it in fact practices
the same old authoritarian control" (109). By focusing on the ways clients
and assistants collude to maintain collaborative-sounding sessions, our
analysis of writing center conversation suggests that despite the assistants'
best efforts to be collaborative, they often assume authoritarian roles. Those
who have worked in writing centers probably do not find it surprising that
the occasional moments of authoritarian instruction creep into mostly collaborative sessions, but perhaps our study's most interesting finding is that
even during these instruction-heavy moments, clients often work hard to uphold the collaborative façade. We were fascinated to find that some clients
even appropriate assistants' language of indirection to ask consultants to be
more direct.

Like Lunsford, we value collaboration's ability to engage active learning, encourage critical thinking, and develop problem-solving skills. Furthermore, we appreciate how collaborative models have emphasized clients'
active participation in writing center sessions and their ownership over the
writing process and product. Yet we hope that our study will point out the
difficulty of implementing a model of peer collaboration within a university writing center that employs graduate student writing assistants. We use
"peer collaboration" to refer to collaboration where authority is assumed to
be distributed equally among participants—where, in the case of the writing center, the graduate student assistant and her client work together as
equals on a specific writing problem that the client brings to the assistant's
attention. Though some writing center scholars have questioned the very
possibility of this definition, we orient our discussion around the idea because it is a central tenet of the USC writing center's Mission Statement and
Philosophy. As these documents from the field suggest, many practical goals

of the writing center—changing perspectives, fostering independence, and bolstering confidence—assume that clients maintain full authority over their work. In each of the sessions we examined, we see clients and assistants colluding to deemphasize the assistants' authority. We found that though both graduate student assistants and writing center clients go to great conversational lengths to appear as equals collaborating, neither seems unaware of the assistant's position of authority, not only in the writing center session, but also over the client's writing.

Methodology: Transcript Analysis

Like Blau, Hall, and Strauss, we analyze writing center transcripts in order to demonstrate the limitations of the collaborative model for client-assistant relationships.[3] Not only do we borrow from linguistics the method of conversation analysis as established by Harvey Sacks, but we also ground our analysis in its theoretical frameworks: McDermott and Tylbor's idea of collusion, Erving Goffman's theories of footing and participant frameworks, which explain how we align ourselves with or relate to other participants during a conversation—both physically and mentally, and J.L. Austin and John Searle's speech act theories, which consider the purposes behind utterances and the performances that accompany socially accepted talk in specific contexts. We look at conversations because we believe it is primarily through talk that clients and tutors construct their social roles and relationships.

We recorded three client-assistant sessions,[4] all led by experienced female graduate students.[5] We focused exclusively on female assistants so that we could more confidently attribute power differentials in communication styles to social roles and not to gender differences.[6] The three clients whose sessions we observed were representative of our diverse clientele, as Table 1 summarizes:

---

[3] Blau, Hall, and Strauss focus on the following linguistic features: questions, echoing, and qualifiers. We, in contrast, focus on directives.

[4] Clients and assistants were invited to participate in this study and given a letter explaining their rights as well as our methodology. Those who volunteered were asked to sign a consent form.

[5] Each of the tutors whom we observed had worked in university writing centers for more than one semester. One was a former assistant director of the writing center.

[6] There is a growing body of scholarship that suggests that the characteristics that have been traditionally associated with "women's language" instead belong to a "language of powerlessness, a condition that can apply to men as well as women" (O'Barr and Atkins 96). See also Marjorie Harnass Goodwin's *He-Said-She-Said: Talk as Social Organization Among Black Children.*

Table 1: Client Profiles

CLIENT	STATUS	GENDER	NATIVE/ NON-NATIVE	PROJECT
Client A	First Year Undergraduate	Female	Native Speaker	Literary Analysis
Client B	Second Year Undergraduate	Male	Native Speaker	Engineering Lab Report
Client C	Graduate Student	Male	Non-Native Speaker	Social Work Case Study

Although we deliberately recorded a sampling of sessions reflective of the diversity of the university's clientele, we recognize that our data are limited to three sessions from one university writing center. Nevertheless, as experienced writing center assistants ourselves, we feel that the sessions we observed are typical of writing centers and that the model of collaboration used at the University of South Carolina is consistent with current practice.

For each session recorded, we transcribed a fifteen to twenty-five minute segment, using a modified version of the transcription conventions developed by Gail Jefferson. Each of the segments we transcribed included "directives," one of the five categories of John Searle's speech acts. As he defines them, directives are, very simply, "attempts . . . by the speaker to get the hearer to do something" (11). We focus on these directives because they especially reveal how speakers position themselves in relation to one another. As Marjorie Goodwin explains, the way that speakers format directives "make[s] possible [and visible, we'd like to add] a variety of social arrangements between participants" (63). Goffman's notion of footing, as Goodwin notes, is particularly useful in describing the ways that speakers use directives to reveal their positions (or footing) in relation to one another:

> [D]irectives provide participants with powerful resources for making public displays about how those present take up a position or 'footing' (Goffman 1981) vis-à-vis each other—how they 'align' themselves in ways relevant to the activities they are collaboratively pursuing. (73)

In other words, directives help us to explain how clients and writing assistants collude in order to position themselves as peers in collaboration. We also chose segments that seemed to point to specific moments in conversations where this model of collaboration falls apart.

As our transcription key (see Appendix Two) demonstrates, we focused our analysis on a small set of linguistic features, and we did not systematically account for nonverbal behaviors, intonational units (the small rhythmic, melodic, or accented elements of spoken language), or prosodic features (how loud, how long, and how high or low the recorded speech sounds were). We acknowledge at the outset, then, that our analysis involves a simplification of complex speech dynamics. As Alessandro Duranti explains, "any kind of inscription is, by definition, *an abstraction in which a complex phenomenon is reduced to some of its constitutive features and transformed for the purpose of further analysis*" (emphasis in original 137).

Maintaining the Collaborative Illusion

Conversational Dysfluency

In order to appear as peer collaborators, the graduate assistants we observed often had to choose their words and directives carefully. They struggled to use embedded, buried, or somewhat de-emphasized directives because they did not want to exert too much power or authority. This regular effort to maintain a collaborative front often led to various types of conversational dysfluency, which was often evidenced in simple uhs and uhms used as fillers as the assistant thought of ways to turn her comments or explicit directives into questions and embedded directives. This conversational dysfluency was especially apparent when Assistant A, who was helping a freshman writer with a literary analysis, began a directive in a very straightforward manner, then stopped and rephrased in more collaborative terms. Assistant A changed her footing within the framework in order to play the role of peer. "Okay let's, let's make a, do you mind if we make a list of the reasons why?"(33–34). She made the same type of footing change later when she stopped and rephrased a statement as a question: "Well, if boys look like boys, then that's why they think {4} If boys look like boys then who does the dad look like?" (163–64).

The assistants we observed also resisted appearing too authoritative by using self-blame to mask their criticism. Often, rather than criticizing a client's unclear writing, the assistant would ask for clarification by blaming herself for not understanding what was said: "Tell me I missed it." Or, as can be seen in this example, Assistant B asks the client to write something down because she is unable to follow it orally: "Assistant B: Okay why don't you try writing that on—I'm not—I don't know that I understand what you mean [maybe you should just write it down]"(85–86). Claiming not to understand what was said becomes an embedded directive to clarify or rethink an idea. Assistant C appears to disagree with what her client is saying at one point; however, she avoids telling him that his sentence is wrong. Instead, she repeatedly claims that she doesn't understand what he is trying to say.

409. **Assistant C:** Now this, I'm not sure about the meaning of the sentence because
410. you say although she was charismatic, she still respected feminism.
411. **Client C:**   Mhm.
412. **Assistant C:** So I'm not sure [what you're,]
413. **Client C:**   [No, uh]
414. **Assistant C:** what are you saying there?
415. **Client C:**   Probably the order is…the egalitarian style [of management]
416. **Assistant C:**   [O:h!]
417. **Client C:** AND feminism.
418. **Assistant C:** OK, let's see: "Although Amonk was a charismatic leader for the
419. entire staff of WRWC," I still don't understand, though, because how come she
420. can't be charismatic *and* respect feminism
421.   [and egalitarianism at the same time]?
422. **Client C:**   [Oh, OK. OK. OK.]
423. **Assistant C:** I'm not sure, what are you trying to say exactly?

Assistant C uses her apparent misunderstanding to guide the client to a
new sentence, all in the form of self-blame, questioning, and collaboration.
Eventually, Client C changes the sentence to clarify the assistant's confusion, yet such an interaction clearly requires a lot of time and energy from
both the assistant, who must maneuver carefully so as to appear nonauthoritative, and from the client, who must guess at the assistant's meaning.
Both client and assistant, in multiple acts of collusion, repeatedly change
their footing or relationship to each other in order to maintain the appearance of collaboration.

Embedded Authorities

Embedded directives also appear when assistants, not wanting to insist upon
their own authority, call on the authority of other actors or agents in the
scene. These embedded actors may be rules—writing center rules, genre
rules, grammar rules—handouts, the text, or even hypothetical critics or situations created by the assistant in order to mask her own authority. For example, trying to get her client to see a particular point in the short story about
which she must write, Assistant A uses what-if situations to direct the client's
thoughts. In the text they discuss, a new father ignores his baby, but the client
has trouble figuring out his motivations. Her own preferred interpretation—
that the baby is adopted, and that the father is uninterested in a child that is
not biologically his own—is challenged by evidence in the story that suggests the mother actually gave birth recently.

61. **Assistant A:** Okay, but there's more. What else would somebody point to if I
     were to say

62. no way this [child was adopted?]

....

76. **Assistant A:** Yeah, I hear what you're saying but you still have to deal with this
     getting out

77. of bed thing. If I were arguing against you I would say oh, she must have been
     pregnant

78. and she was in bed giving birth.

Assistant A uses the hypothetical "somebody" in one effort to get her point across indirectly and the hypothetical situation of arguing against the client to make the same point a few lines later. Assistant B uses the same technique and creates a hypothetical situation for her client.

49. **Assistant B:** Okay, so given all of that and on those things that you did have to

50. figure out, um how would you write in a sentence what you think, if you need to

51. sum up in one or two sentences what the basic results were for the lab, what

52. would you say?

Though the assistant poses the question hypothetically, the client does, in fact, have to sum up his ideas in a sentence if he is to follow the assignment guidelines.

The assignment becomes another way to embed directives and call on embedded authorities during the session. For instance, Assistant B begins her session by asking the client if he was present in class the day they were given a "checklist of what each part needed" (7–8). Later she pulls out a handout to guide their session and quotes from it to give the client instructions. To use another example, in her session, Assistant A tries to get the client to decide who the baby in the story looks like, as well as the significance of this idea to the characters involved. She turns to the authority of the text.

151. (**Assistant A** reading over story and sort of mumbling as she reads) What else
     do they

152. say? (Reading) "But he has to look like somebody." Okay. If he has to look like

153. somebody who must he look like?

The assistant locates a place in the text to direct the client to the next point as she builds her outline for her paper. The authority of the text allows the assistant to criticize the student's writing without compromising her appearance as peer.

The embedded authorities used by the assistants in these particular writing center sessions illustrate how writers and assistants collude to uphold an image of peer collaboration. In the case of the assistants, it seems especially important to have an outside authority that they can cite as the actor insisting on a change (of mind, style, content, or grammar) on the part of the client. When they can rely on such rules, handouts, or conventions, assistants become much more straightforward and explicit with their directives, although they still may couch them in interrogative terms. For example, Assistant A agrees with what her client says but then points out the rules for making her case: "But then you know every time you say something like that you have to point, and quote" (116–17).

Assistant C, who works with a non-native speaker, points out several grammatical rules, some in the form of questions, "You want to make that plural?" (287) and others as statements, "I would say 'due to,' no 'its'"(297) or "you don't need an article here (pointing to 'the')" (335). However, after directly pointing out grammar rules that applied to the client's paper, the assistant seems to catch herself not operating as a collaborator and offers lengthy explanations in order to excuse her directness.

359. **Assistant C:** The easiest way to do something like this, to, whenever

360. you're constructing a sentence like this, is going to be to put her name

361. first: "However, Barbara Armonk" comma "a staff member" comma

362. "became a leader."=

363. **Client C:**   =OK.

364. **Assistant C:** That's an easier way to construct a sentence like that.

365. **Client C:**   OK.

366. **Assistant C:** It's just a little clearer.

The client, however, appears to accept her authority, and the assistant continues to use explicit directives about issues of grammar.

Inclusive Pronouns

Just as the graduate writing center assistants in this study use embedded authorities and lapse into sentence dysfluency to uphold the myth of collaboration, they use inclusive pronouns to suggest that the client is actively involved in issuing directives. This use of inclusive pronouns is the most simplistic, yet perhaps most representative method of disguising the assistant's authority. In these cases the assistant issues veiled directives, telling her client what to do while concealing her authority through the use of inclusive language. For example, when an assistant uses the phrase "We decided . . ." rather than "I decided . . . ," she insists that the decision is a joint one. Assistant A colludes in this way when she tries to help her client think through another significant detail of the short story about the new baby. Because the client isn't confident about a definitive interpretation, she prefers to leave the issue unaddressed. In trying to guide the client toward a reading validated by textual evidence, Assistant A struggles to reconcile her authority with her commitment to collaborative pedagogy.

86. **Client A:** [okay]
87. **Assistant A:** [okay] Erica. We have to get back, to the question of why.
88. **Client A:** *I don't know why.=*
89. **Assistant A:** =and you said=
90. **Client A:** =That's what I don't know and I don't have any support=
91. **Assistant A:** =okay, wait, you have support for the, you said that you don't think it's his
92. child, and what I'm pointing out, trying to point out to you is that you said that you, you
93. didn't want to say that this is definitely, the interpretation, if you can't think of any other
94. possibilities of why, then definitely present your interpretation as this is the way to read it.
95. Cause it sounds like we can't come up with any possibilities.

Rather than directly telling the client to assert that the baby is not biologically the father's child, Assistant A refers to previous client input. "You didn't want to say that this is definitely, the interpretation" (line 93). Yet she cannot avoid issuing a clear directive. ". . . if you can't think of any other possibilities of why, then definitely present your interpretation as this is the way to read it" (lines 93–94). Assistant A seemingly realizes that she has violated the collaborative paradigm, and she offers next an inclusive pronoun to repair the interaction. "Cause it sounds like we can't come up with any possibilities" (line 95). On the surface, this use of "we" shifts the responsibility for generating other possible readings to the collaborative pair.

At a subconscious level at least, clients seem quite aware of the linguistic maneuverings of their assistants. In fact, as Client A demonstrates later in the session, clients often use the collaborative language of their writing center assistants to direct the session according to their own agendas and to mask disagreement they have with the assistants who work with them. Here Client A uses inclusive language to critique the assistant's persistence in supporting a close reading.

61. **Assistant A:** Okay, but there's more. What else would somebody point to if I were to say
62. no way this [child was adopted?]

63. **Client A:** [Oh yeah,] /we were discussing how/ she just got out of bed and stuff, *but*

64. *that could mean a lot of stuff.* just don't want to think that, it's because she's had a baby,

65. because my mind wanders, and *I* would think that, I mean it's just not necessarily

66. mean that. People just take the literal value of it, and it could mean like, she was, you

67. know like, so overjo::yed, she was, I don't know, she was so excited that she finally had

68. a baby boy, [you know like]

In this example, Client A uses inclusive pronouns and an embedded authority to introduce her own understanding of the mother's behavior. "We were discussing how she just got out of bed and stuff, but that could mean a lot of stuff" (lines 63–64). She is in fact rejecting Assistant A's reading that the mother had recently given birth, and she subtly criticizes her assistant for being too literal. "People just take the literal value of it, and it could mean like, she was, you know like so overjoyed . . ." (lines 66–67). The collusion that takes place in this specific example is complicated. On one hand, the fact that the client adopts the inclusive language of the assistant shows how both participants jump through linguistic hoops to uphold the image of peer collaboration. Not wanting to act without the others' approval, both the assistant and the client avoid expressing dissent by preferring pronouns like "we" that imply consensus. This seems to suggest that the collaborative model may inhibit clients' and assistants' expression of disagreement and conflict. Furthermore, no matter how perceptively the client adopts collaborative language and subtly moves towards issues of her choosing, the session is never out of her control for long.

Suspending the Collaborative Illusion

In the sessions we observed, clients and assistants collude with the institutional edict that they should act as peers and that writing center sessions should be collaborative. Not wanting to disrupt this illusion, clients adopt assistants' style of speaking, which includes the use of embedded authorities and inclusive pronouns. Though clients and assistants are often successful at constructing and maintaining the illusion of collaboration, there are also moments when the façade of collaboration is ripped away. Two moments in the conversation between Assistant C and Client C reveal such a breakdown of the collaborative illusion.

Both transcript excerpts are taken from the first ten minutes of the session when the client, a non-native speaker and graduate student, shared with the assistant his professor's comments about his writing. In the first example, Client C responds to the assistant's question, "What did, um, what did he (referring to the professor) think of your, what did he say about the last case study that you turned in?":

38. **Client C:**   [He] doesn't want to give us a specific, you know, this
39.   is a example, blah-blah-blah-blah-blah. He doesn't, you know, he tries to
40.   avoid, uh, formulate /his answer/.
41. **Assistant C:** OK.
42. **Client C:** That's why everybody gets frustrated: "I don't under[stand]
43. **Assistant C:**   [OK]
44. **Client C:**   *how* we're-
45. **Assistant C:** So you're saying he, his comments tend to be ambiguous—
46.   other students [[think]]
47. **Client C:** [[Right. Then-]]
48. **Assistant C:** that his comments are ambiguous as well? Oh, [wow].=
49. **Client C:**   [*THEN*] he
50.   kept saying /after class/, your analysis must be *completely specific*=
51. **Assistant C:** =[OK]
52. **Client C:** [So,] it's like a major contradiction, you know?
53. **Assistant C:** OK. [[OK]]
54. **Client C:** [[His]] words and his actions. What are you deman-
55.   demanding? What?
56. **Assistant C:** Yeah…I think a lot of professors have that syndrome.
57.   (laughing)
58. **Client C:** Yeah, *THEN*, like, it's like in the classroom when we, when we
59.   have a really specific/case in mind/=
60. **Assistant C:** =uh [huh?]
61. **Client C:** [/ask him] why,/ a question about, OK, in *this* case
62.   how we can, you know, state the /conclusion/? [How]
63. **Assistant C:**   [OK]
64. **Client C:**   we can /come up with/ the solution/? And when even we ask the
65.   professor, he say, "Look, I try to avoid to answer the question."
66. **Assistant C:** Oh, 'cause he doesn't want to feed you the answer that he
67.   wants to hear. That's what he's try, I think, well that's what *I* would think
68.   he's doing. He wants you to, figure it out on your own instead of, but I can
69.   see why you're frustrated.
70. **Client C:**   Yeah.
71. **Assistant C:** Yeah=

72. **Client C:** =But that's why like, OK, yeah, I want to know, your
73. answer is? I know the case there is no right or wrong answer=
74. **Assistant C:**   =Right, right, right=
75. **Client C:**   =Right?
76. **Assistant C:** Right=
77. **Client C:**   =But still, like, I want to know more like experienced
78. social worker's perspective, you [know? I don't know why]
79. **Assistant C:**   [Yea:h]
80. **Client C:** but he doesn't show it. But why? (whispering emphatically)
81. <Why?
82. **Assistant C:** O:h. So, so other students are having trouble, too?

In this excerpt, Client C complains about his professor's refusal to provide specific direction and clarification about course assignments. As long as the assistant sympathizes with the client's perspective (lines 45–46, 48: "So you're saying he, his comments tend to be ambiguous—other students [[think]] that his comments are ambiguous as well?"), he gives her verbal assurances (line 47: "Right"; line 58 "Yeah."). Yet when the assistant begins to identify with the professor, whose agenda—much like hers—is to get the student to think for himself (lines 66–68), Client C withholds his affirmation. The assistant's apparent conversational dysfluency signals that she recognizes that she has—in identifying with the professor's, not the student's, perspective—somehow disrupted the illusion of peer collaboration. She, therefore, quickly changes her footing in order to realign herself with the client: "but I can see why you're frustrated" (69).

In order to protect the illusion of collaboration and peer-to-peer interaction, the client corrects the assistant who, by identifying with the professor, threatens this fiction.[7] Not until after the assistant repositions herself as a peer does the client offer her the affirmation, "Yeah," which signals that despite this momentary disruption, they are going to continue as "peers." This is, in fact, what they do for a few minutes until the collaborative model again breaks down.

Still relaying his professor's feedback on the case studies that he and Assistant C had been working on, Client C creates another analogy that demonstrates even more dramatically than the first example how the model of collaboration breaks down. This section of conversation follows the client's

---

[7] Incidentally, the client's words can also be interpreted as a means through which the client directs the assistant to be more explicit. Using the indirect communication styles that the assistant herself has modeled, and the client no doubt internalized through previous sessions with her, the client can be evoking the figure of the professor in order to safely displace his criticism. In other words, though he is explicitly directing his frustration at the professor who "avoid[s]…answer[ing] the question[s]," he may be extending his criticism to the assistant as

rather startling revelation that his writing is not the cause of his unsatisfactory grades:

170. **Assistant C:** OK. {3}. OK. {3}. It must be nice to know that it's not
171. the writing that's the problem anymore, though. That's got to be half of
172. the, I mean, that's got to be relief, I think.
173. **Client C:** You think so be[cause-]
174. **Assistant C:**   [Yeah, definitely.]

....

185. **Client C:** And, but, I think the problems with my struggling is more,
186. /is real/ more problematic because otherwise it's directly related to social
187. work skills, uh...
188. **Assistant C:** Oh, I see. Yeah. Well, I don't know if I would go that far
189. because if other students are struggling, too, you know, I mean, if you
190. were one of the only ones who was struggling with this, stating the
191. problem, then maybe, but if other students are struggling, too, it sounds
192. like everybody's kind of, you know, like this is just kind of hard material,
193.   [you know?]
194. **Client C:** [O:r] the, the instructor's expectations are so high, [[that-]]
195. **Assistant C:**   [[perhaps,
196. yeah, yeah.]] So I wouldn't, I wouldn't, you know, ah internalize it so
197. much. Just be patient, and I would think that you'll catch on to
198.   [what he wants after a while. You know?]
199. **Client C:** [Yeah@, RIGHT. Right. Exactly,] you sound like a social
200. worker= (laughing)
201. **Assistant C:** =I do? (a pause) I sound like a social worker?
202. **Client C:** ha ha. Yeah=
203. **Assistant C:** =hmmm.
204. **Client C:** /?/
205. **Assistant C:** Mmhm.
206. **Client C:** /And like/ we have a formula, um, /in taking in Client Care,
207. who has a problem/ (feigning a sweet, concerned voice) <"OK, you know,
208. tell me what your problem — "/Well, actually, / Then, we lead and then
209. they give us some detailed information, then we have a for[mula,]
210. **Assistant C:**   [uh huh]
211. **Client C:** that's like "please, tell me more" (laughing).
212. **Assistant C:** Right.
213. **Client C:** keep going, leading, [leading]

214. **Assistant C:**   [right]

215. **Client C:** leading, [[you know.]]

216. **Assistant C:** [[right]] You have to really pull teeth=

217. **Client C:** =Right.

218. **Assistant C:** To get it out of them. Yeah.

219. **Client C:** Well, you must be very used to it. Became a, become a second

220. nature.

221. **Assistant C:** Yeah. {8}. Is that what this wh-, whole course is? Is all,

222. all you do is analyze cases?

In this case, almost a reversal of the first, Client C disrupts the myth of collaboration by beating the assistant at her own game, so to speak. By telling her after she has tried to placate him that "[she] sounds like a social worker" (line 199), the client is, in effect, turning the tables on her, telling her that he knows the rules of her game and also insinuating (even more so in lines 206–209) that he knows her strategies for helping him follow a formulaic procedure. It is no wonder, then, that the assistant does not join the client in laughter and rather indicates disapproval of his antics by responding coolly with "hmmm" and "Mmhm." Sensing that she is offended, the client tries to defuse the situation by describing at length the procedure that social workers use to get their clients to talk.

In light of Client C's analogy, lines 200–215 assume a double meaning: in these lines, the client and assistant both used the figure of the social worker to express their frustration with their respective roles and with the myth of collaboration. In lines 216 and 218 ("You have to really pull teeth to get it out of them"), the assistant not only acknowledges the difficult role of the social worker, but she (having just been compared to a social worker herself) also expresses her frustrations with her own role; she implies that trying to get the "right" answer out of clients is like pulling teeth. And in line 219, the client adds his jab—that this method of indirection has become the assistant's "second nature." After the awkward silence that follows this comment, the assistant regains her composure by shifting topics.

The client's veiled directive and the assistant's covert frustrations with her role as "collaborator" demonstrate how maintaining the idea of peer collaboration is difficult for both parties: the client is frustrated because he wants the assistant, just as he wants his professor, to be more direct and to avoid formulaic responses to his writing. The assistant, in turn, also expresses the difficulty of her position. When in the first example she identifies with the client's professor, Assistant C articulates the rationale behind her strategy of indirection—that it makes the client think for himself. And in the second example, she expresses (albeit from a position of safety) her frustration with that position—that trying to direct the client while masking her authority and power is an exhausting process not unlike pulling teeth.

At both of these moments in the peer-tutor session, the collaborative construct has collapsed for client as well as assistant. Yet in each case, one speaker (in the first case, the client, and in the second the assistant) is able to temporarily repair the break so that the session can resume under the guise of "peer collaboration."

* * *

Our intention in this chapter has been to demonstrate how assistants and clients invest in the construct of peer collaboration as perpetuated by writing center mission statements, assistant training sessions, and writing center scholarship. The graduate assistant goes to extraordinary linguistic lengths to disguise her authority and to appear as a peer collaborator—displacing her authority to third parties and institutions (the handout, grammar rules, genre conventions, the text) and using inclusive pronouns. Given the difficulty of her task, it is no wonder that her speech is often marked by considerable conversational dysfluency. The client also plays a role in maintaining this (appearance of) collaboration; she/he, too, adopts inclusive pronouns and embedded authority. Despite the earnest efforts of both parties, and in spite of the good intentions motivating these writing center pedagogies, peer collaboration breaks down, even at the linguistic level. At marked points in writing center sessions, both clients and assistants recognize that the model of peer collaboration is incredibly difficult to uphold, that it can be exhausting and frustrating, that it can stifle honest critique and open disagreement, and that it often results in formulaic responses to clients' needs.

We would like, therefore, to add our voice along with others like Blau, Hall, and Strauss, Clark, and Shamoon and Burns to the growing concern with the model of collaboration in writing center practice. While peer collaboration, in theory, is a laudable ideal, it is often tenuous in practice. This is particularly true within the hierarchical institution of the university that houses the writing center in which assistants must strike a delicate balance between their simultaneous roles of "peers" and experts. As Lunsford puts it, true collaboration only exists when "[s]tudents, tutors, teachers...really need one another to carry out common goals" (111). These conversation analyses suggest that it may be frustrating at best and misleading at worst to ignore the power and knowledge disparity inherent to most client-graduate student assistant relationships. Our study suggests that the model of peer-collaboration may be flawed for both clients and assistants and that an improved model would empower graduate student assistants by allowing them, when appropriate, to draw upon their expertise and authority while also empowering writers by allowing them to direct the session and to disagree more openly with the assistants who work with them.

Works Cited

Austin, J.L. *How to Do Things With Words.* Oxford: Clarendon Press, 1962.

Blau, Susan R., John Hall, and Tracy Strauss. "Exploring the Tutor/Client Conversations: A Linguistic Analysis." *The Writing Center Journal* 19.1 (1998): 19–48.

Bokser, Julie A. "Peer Tutoring and Gorgias: Acknowledging Aggression in the Writing Center." *The Writing Center Journal* 21.1 (2001): 21–34.

Clark, Irene. "Perspectives on the Directive/Non-Directive Continuum in the Writing Center." *The Writing Center Journal* 22.1 (2001): 33–58.

Duranti, Alessandro. *Linguistic Anthropology.* Cambridge: Cambridge UP, 1997.

Goodwin, Marjorie H. *He-Said-She-Said: Talk as Social Organization Among Black Children.* Bloomington: Indiana UP, 1990.

Goffman, Erving. "Footing." *Forms of Talk.* Philadelphia: U of Pennsylvania P, 1981. 124–57.

Lunsford, Andrea. "Collaboration, Control, and the Idea of a Writing Center." *Landmark Essays on Writing Centers.* Ed. Christina Murphy and Joe Law. Davis, CA: Hermagoras Press, 1995. 109–15.

McDermott, R.P., and H. Tylbor. "On the Necessity of Collusion in Conversation." *The Dialogic Emergence of Culture.* Ed. D. Tedlock and B. Mannheim. Urbana: U of Illinois P, 1995. 218–36.

O'Barr, William M., and Bowman K. Atkins. "'Women's Language' or 'Powerless Language'?" *Women and Language in Literature and Society.* Ed. Sally McConnell-Ginet, Ruth Barker, and Nelly Furman. New York: Praeger, 1980. 93–107.

Sacks, Harvey, Emanuel A. Schegloff, and Gail Jefferson. "A Simplest Systematics for the Organization of Turn-Taking for Conversation." *Language* 50 (1974): 696–735.

Searle, John R. "A Classification of Illocutionary Acts." *Language in Society* 5 (1976): 1–23.

Shamoon, Linda K., and Deborah H. Burns. "A Critique of Pure Tutoring." *The Writing Center Journal* 15.2 (1995): 134–151.

Writing Center at USC. *Staff Handbook.* Columbia: University of South Carolina, 1998.

Appendix One

Philosophy[8]

For excellence, the presence of others is always required.—Hannah Arendt

The University of South Carolina Writing Center is a place for collaboration, one where any writer can come to think and talk about writing. We view writing as a process and writing sessions as an exchange of ideas about individual writers' processes. These writing sessions are based on a complementary expertise model, where, through conversation, writing assistants and writers (the clients) combine their individual knowledge and skills to improve a written text. This teamwork can change writers' perspectives about the writing process, thereby emphasizing the benefits of collaboration and feedback and transforming the usually solo ritual of writing.

Treating the writing session as a collaborative effort (and explaining it as such to clients) fosters independence by teaching clients to engage in conversation about writing with people other than writing assistants and to have confidence in their own abilities. And it encourages student clients to welcome the involvement of their teachers. To include teachers in the conversation taking place in the writing center, writing assistants provide detailed, descriptive narratives about the session to teachers. The collaborative nature of the sessions also precludes proofreading and editing activities.

Since we value the positive effect collaboration has on writing and respect the background and expertise of our clients, those who work with clients are called "writing assistants." We prefer this term over "tutor" and "consultant," both of which imply a hierarchy in which the tutor/consultant has privileged knowledge to share with the client. We value what both assistant and client bring to the conversation about writing. Also, we have chosen "assistant" to emphasize the service that the writing center provides: an experienced staff to help clients talk about and improve writing.

Ultimately, the goal of the writing center is to help produce better writers. We think participating in clients' writing processes—through sharing ideas about writing and the writing process, working together to improve specific texts—will achieve this end.

---

[8] The Philosophy and Mission Statement of the writing center at the University of South Carolina as stated in the *Staff Handbook* given to assistants at orientation.

Mission Statement

The Writing Center's central mission is to enlarge and enrich the writing experience of members of the University of South Carolina community and the greater community. To fulfill this mission, the Writing Center staff

- In one-on-one sessions, works with university students, faculty, and staff as well as members of the greater community with every stage of the writing process

- In cooperation with Housing and Residential Services, uses satellite centers to enlarge the writing community and to improve accessibility to our services

- Through seminars, workshops, and consultations, advises and mentors university and community educators incorporating writing into their classes

- Advises faculty and instructors on designing effective writing assignments and on responding to student writing effectively and efficiently

- Fosters outreach programs targeted at elementary, middle, and high school students and their teachers

- Initiates and sponsors research on writing and writing center theory and practice

- Responds to questions from the Writer's Hotline, by phone and email

- Maintains a small library on writing theory and praxis

Appendix Two

Transcription Key

"words"	Quoted passages were read verbatim from the client's paper.
Italics	Italicized words were given special emphasis when spoken.
<u>Underline</u>	Words underlined were spoken rapidly.
(in parentheses)	Any comments that were not part of the recorded conversation are enclosed in parentheses. Usually, these comments describe non-verbal behaviors that the observer noted as she recorded the conversation.
/words/	Any words surrounded by backslashes indicate speech that the recorder was uncertain about. The approximate content is documented.
/?/	This symbol denotes an utterance that was unintelligible.
<	This less-than sign indicates decreased volume.
ALL CAPS	Capitals indicate increased volume.
[words]	Brackets are used to indicate places where speakers' words overlapped.
=	The equal sign indicates "latching," places where there is no interval between the end of one person's turn and the beginning of the next speaker's turn.
{#}	Pauses of three or more seconds are documented in whole second duration within brackets. Pauses of less than three seconds are considered natural and are marked with commas.
:	Colons indicate that the vowel or consonant sound immediately preceding was noticeably lengthened.
-	Dashes mark sudden cut-offs or interruptions of the current sound.
@	This sign marks words that were punctuated by laughter.

CHAPTER 9

Grounds for Growth:

A Territorialist Perspective on Graduate Students in the Writing Center

Lucas Niiler

Introduction

A large blue swivel chair sits behind the receptionist's desk at the entrance to the University of Texas at Tyler writing center. This chair was ordered by Karen, a former graduate tutor I hired not only for her tutoring ability but also her clerical acumen. Karen sat in the chair behind the main desk in the writing center, the desk that all clients must pass by upon entrance, the desk that similarly commands a sweeping view of the entire room. Karen sat in the chair to take appointments, conduct online and telephone tutorials, and conduct the business of her daily shift. Now that Karen has graduated, other tutors—at first, almost tentatively—have begun sitting in that chair. I never sit in that chair. The site is exceptionally well-marked; it's as if that chair bears a plaque with Karen's name on it. My reticence may in part be explained by Karen's characteristic expression whenever I entered the writing center on her shift. She would look up at me with an expression that asked, "Can I help you?"

Karen's behavior and my response can be theorized in part by Cornelis Bakker and Marianne Bakker-Rabdau, who use the term "territoriality" to designate "the ubiquitous human need to control social space [or territory]" (3). A social space, or territory, can be defined as "the object of ownership" (Bakker and Bakker-Rabdau 3). Such territory can be further classified as either "psychological" or "action" space. For Bakker and Bakker-Rabdau, psychological space is identified with how much influence one person has over another (18), such as an employer over a subordinate, a parent over a child, or a teacher over a student. Action space, in turn, refers to those arenas within which an individual can act autonomously by "[exerting] control, [making] decisions, [exercising] expertise, and [taking] responsibility" (23). Such spaces include classrooms, offices, and, as I will discuss, writing centers.

Yet determining just who controls what space can be unclear, as "territories are primarily cognitive constructions [that] can only be perceived through the markers used by people to delimit and identify them" (Jordan para. 9). If we are able, however, to observe and understand a person's so-called "territorial behaviors," then we can determine if a territory does in fact exist. These behaviors include the *acquisition* of more territory; *warning* others away from possible incursions on that territory; *defense* of a given territory; and the *marking* of territory. Territoriality, notes Robert Sack, "is the primary spatial form power takes" (26). Territorial behaviors of acquisition, warning, defense and marking are therefore considered applications of power. And because the exercise of power so often occurs within the context of a struggle for psychological or action space, territorial behaviors are often discussed in terms of weaponry. Put another way, territorial "weapons" manifest distinct territorial "behaviors": we wield specific weapons of *definition, self-definition, beneficence,* and *seduction* as we struggle to acquire space, mark it, warn others away from it, and defend it.

Certainly, writing center administrators are very much attuned to issues of territoriality in their daily work, as much of that work involves the acquisition, marking, warning, and defense of the psychological and action space constituted by the writing center. What room or rooms will the writing center occupy? What source will fund the writing center? What kind of funding will the writing center receive? Who will staff the writing center? And what will the writing center determine as protocol, both in terms of tutoring technique and in terms of administration? How will the writing center contend with the inevitable conflicts that can arise over misunderstandings of its philosophy, mission and goals? How will it defend its position as a tutoring, as opposed to an editing, facility? To be sure, these are perennial concerns of writing center scholarship (see, for example, Carino "Writing;" Ede; Grimm; Lunsford; North "Idea," "Revisiting"). Writing center work, in short, is fraught with daily power struggles—some of which are easily negotiated and ameliorated, while others are protracted, often perilous.

Here I use a territorialist perspective to examine how graduate students are prepared for professional, academic life through working in The University of Texas at Tyler writing center.[1] I am particularly intrigued by the territorial behaviors they employ—and the territorial weapons they deploy—

---

[1] I will rely primarily on the work of Bakker and Bakker-Rabdau for this piece, although the reader is encouraged to consult the more comprehensive explanations of territoriality available in the work of Robert Ardrey (*The Social Contract: A Personal Inquiry into the Evolutionary Sources of Order and Disorder,* Dell, 1970; and *The Territorial Imperative: A Personal Inquiry into the Animal Origins of Property and Nations,* Kodansha, 1997); Robert Sack (*Conceptions of Space in Social Thought: A Geographic Perspective,* U of Minnesota P, 1980; and *Homo Geographicus: A Framework for Action, Awareness, and Moral Concern,* Hopkins UP, 1997); and Ralph B. Taylor (*Human Territorial Functioning: An Empirical, Evolutionary Perspective on Individual and Small Group Territorial Cognition, Behavior, and Consequences,* Cambridge UP, 1988).

in the exercise of their daily work, work that benefits their tutoring clients as it augments their professional growth. A close examination of these be-. haviors and weapons suggests that graduate tutors in fact learn to command a great deal of power in the writing center. Not quite faculty, but well-beyond their undergraduate degrees, UTT's graduate tutors are managers who, in effect, direct on a daily basis the action space—the actual writing center facility itself—set aside for them by the university administration and writing center director. In addition, they command, through their expertise as writers, the psychological space comprised by the tutorial; this writing center, in fact, promotes and celebrates the expertise of its graduate tutors. Such a command is an integral part of the ongoing development of graduate students' identities as professional academics. Their professional identities, in short, are contingent in large part on the power they wield and the psychological territory they control.

I should note at the outset that readers may associate the territorialist terminology I will use in this chapter as metaphors for violence and war (for example, I use the term "weapons" frequently within situations I clearly delineate as rife with conflict). Some of my rhetoric may also suggest that I am celebrating graduate tutors' expertise at the expense of student learning: that in fact I am eschewing, even stigmatizing, tutor-student collaboration in the writing center. These are not at all my intentions. I am working, rather, in the same vein as Jason Palmeri and Peter Carino, who closely consider the role of power and authority in peer tutorials. "Tutorials," notes Carino, "depend on authority and power,"

> authority about the nature of the writing and the power to proceed from or resist what that authority says. Either tutor and student must share authority, producing a pleasant but rare collaborative peer situation...or one or the other must have it, and in writing centers the one with it is more often the tutor...Writing centers should not be ashamed of this fact. ("Power" 106–107)

I am seeking, in short, a theoretical articulation of power and authority that will help writing centers more fully, accurately, and, above all, honestly define what I take to be their considerable institutional expertise: an expertise that I do not view as violent or threatening but instead as a means of significant opportunity for graduate students. Expertise need not mean the appropriation of a student's draft or a reversion to a "top-down," non-collaborative means of instruction. A tutor's authority—his or her expertise— can augment a student's learning experience by helping that student learn what Palmeri terms "self-confidence, independent thought, and the ability to manipulate academic discourse" (10). This essay, then, traces the development of the power and authority through an examination of the territorial behaviors of *acquisition, warning, defense,* and *marking* as they are present in the work of graduate tutors in the UTT writing center. These behaviors, as I have noted above, are manifest through territorial "weapons" of *definition, self-definition, beneficence,* and *seduction:* weapons that, as we will see, "[help] students achieve their own authority as writers in a power laden environment such as the university" (Carino, "Power" 113).

Behavior One: Acquisition

The writing center constitutes the actual physical or action space within which graduate tutors work. The writing center is a space within which tutors feel a sense of "familiarity, attachment, and safety," an "area in which [they] consider it [their] prerogative to act, exert control, make decisions, exercise…expertise, and take responsibility" (Bakker and Bakker-Rabdau 3, 23). Karen[2], the graduate tutor noted above, describes her work in the UTT writing center in territorialist terms as an experience that enabled her transition from student to faculty member. She notes that her tutoring helped her claim, or acquire, the psychological space of faculty influence.

> I think that because I was allowed to become a tutor, faculty could see me as something beyond a mere student. I was given the opportunity to develop my authority and my teaching style in the writing center, so the university was more comfortable with me entering the classroom. (Keith).

Karen also notes that her writing center experience enabled her to better understand the action space of both the classroom and the student-generated essay. Tutoring provided her with "an insider's glimpse into faculty territory," a glimpse that she continues to parlay as she defines her own teaching style which is based on the teaching strategies she observed in the writing center.

> As a tutor, I heard all the gossip, rants and raves—everything instructors did right or wrong in the eyes of their students. As a result, I was able to begin selecting those behaviors and weapons I would use when I moved into the classroom. (Keith)

Karen's classroom teaching, in sum, is the stuff of which strong writing center practice is made. True to her tutoring background, she sits at eye-level with her students, directly instructs them in productive peer-tutoring techniques, and considers the primary texts of her composition courses to be her students' own texts. Yet Karen's experience is itself grounded in a series of acquisitions and definitions that predate her hiring. The action space of the uni-

---

[2] All tutors interviewed for this study gave informed, oral consent to participate.

versity writing center was defined and acquired by the university administration when—as is so often the case—faculty clamored for stronger writing instruction that might ease students' transitions from area community colleges to UTT (this, at a time when UTT was solely an "upper-division" campus). The writing center itself is a clearly defined and centrally located space, a former seminar room located a brief distance down the hall from the English department offices. I was hired on a tenure-track line to develop and direct the writing center, and upon my arrival on campus, I hired graduate tutors to staff the facility. The departmental location, affiliation and directorship is indeed deliberate, and, in fact, is a significant revision of the first writing center at this institution which was located far from the main course of pedestrian traffic, staffed by undergraduates, and poorly promoted. Before it served its first client, our writing center had acquired space and academic status: both action space and psychological space that translated to a kind of instant credibility, especially when contrasted with the previous center's lack of credibility.

To this end, the UTT writing center does not follow a strict "peer tutor" approach. If this were in fact the case, the tutorial staff would be primarily comprised of undergraduates, as undergraduates comprise the vast majority of our clientele. Graduate tutors provide the most experienced writing help on campus, as they have had the most exposure to various writing assignments across the disciplines: in particular, theses and dissertations, which are periodically the topics of tutorials. Graduate students are typically ten- to twenty-years older than most undergraduates and demonstrate a commensurate level of maturity and responsibility. Many of UTT's graduate students have significant work experience, such as teaching, professional writing, and public relations work that can be considered enormously beneficial to good tutoring. The combination of an experienced director supervising a highly qualified staff is a deployment of the territorial weapon of definition. There is no doubt: the action space of the writing center is defined, controlled, and maintained by professionals with significant expertise in the field of writing.

To an extent, graduate tutors' psychological space has also been proscribed: this, in the form of the writing center's "Philosophy, Mission, and Goals" statements (Niiler, "Information for Students"). These statements, while delineating in some detail the underlying assumptions of writing center work, do not entirely dictate the work of the tutorial. The exact wording extends to the tutors a great deal of Burkean "agency": the freedom and ability to act, to discover and develop their own best tutoring practices through the ongoing process of reflective practice. The writing center's statement of philosophy reads, in part,

> that individual writers work in unique, nonformulaic ways; that each
> student writer requires individualized writing instruction; and that
> writing-intensive coursework can and should be an integral part of a

comprehensive liberal arts education. (Niiler, "Information for Faculty")

This philosophy is an underlying assumption, a touchstone. It allows graduate tutors the freedom to use the territorial weapon of self-definition to maintain control of the psychological space represented by the writing center. One manifestation of this weapon of self-definition is rhetorical choice. A tutor will not, for example, position herself as an editor through the use of "hard" imperatives or commands, such as "Change this phrasing" or "Move this block of text." A tutor will not claim the action or psychological space of the classroom by contesting an instructor's writing assignment or offering her view on the quality of that writing assignment or the quality of a client's draft. Yet tutors will employ specific rhetorical strategies to define themselves as consultants, even as they retain authority as more experienced writers. They repeat key points a tutee raises and are quick with praise terms ("Well done"; "That's great"). They employ the subjunctive mood and "soft" imperatives through phrases such as "It would help if" and "I might suggest."[3] They encourage tutees with affirmative statements such as "That's interesting" and "You put it so well." And they ask open-ended questions that encourage speculation on the part of tutees: questions beginning with "What if," "Can you," "How might you," and, of course "Why" and "How."[4] Underlying these self-defining rhetorical choices, however, is the tutors' authority as the most experienced writers on campus. The graduate tutor, the expert student writer, acquires the action space of the student text by demonstrating—through conversational, collaborative tutoring strategy—how that text might be improved. The more a given student text needs revision, the more action space the tutor has. The student writer, in turn, concedes psychological space to the graduate tutor not only by acknowledging the need for that tutor's expertise, but also by making changes in her draft based on the tutor's suggestions.

Tutors additionally deploy the territorial weapon of definition as they promote the writing center in classroom presentations, in which they designate acceptable uses of the center ("brainstorming," "reviewing," "helping," "discussing") while designating other activities ("editing," "proofreading," "guaranteeing a grade") as unacceptable, even dishonest. This definition process has been noted by Carino, who in his 2002 rhetorical analysis of the promotional literature of several writing centers, argues that such materials "[struggle] against Western culture's conceptions of individual authorship and American education's ideas of ethics—both of which are culturally ingrained in many faculty and students" ("Reading"

---

[3] For a linguistic analysis and critique of these verbal techniques, see Brooke Rollins, Trixie Smith, and Evelyn Westbrook, this volume.

[4] These observations are derived from Niiler's ongoing action research project focusing on face-saving strategies in writing center tutorials.

100). Such definition is largely proactive—or, to speak in terms of territorial weaponry, a pre-emptive strike against popular misconceptions of the writing center's role in the drafting process. A particularly effective classroom demonstration at UTT involves two tutors who role-play two tutorials. The first depicts a student arriving at the writing center, dropping off her paper, and returning an hour later to pick up a thoroughly edited copy. The tutor sends the student off with a guarantee: "Your paper is sure to get an 'A'!" The second scenario depicts a student sitting down with a tutor to review an assignment and discuss a first draft of that assignment; this demonstration features many of the collaborative tropes listed above. Students viewing both skits laugh at the first depiction of a tutorial, and remain largely amenable to the strategies depicted in the second. It is as if students understand their popular conception of the writing center as an editing facility as intellectually bankrupt, while conceding the value of the more challenging, collaborative model. In territorialist terms, students concede the psychological space of the tutorial to the tutors. Through the marked contrast between scenarios, writing center protocol is introduced.

Beneficence and seduction are additional weapons utilized in the act of acquisition of the psychological space of the writing center. Beneficence is implicit in the rhetoric used to define and promote the writing center: tutors promise professional assistance with difficult writing projects. Tutors promise to "support, not punish" (Niiler, "Information for Students"). Tutors greet students warmly, professionally. Small wonder, then, that students sometimes assume that the often much older tutor has become their adopted parent; the tutor, after all, has kindly promised to help the student with her writing. There is a form of seduction at work here as well, a territorial weapon Bakker and Bakker-Rabdau term "the creation of an expectation of some greater good" (190). This is a promise that may be misconstrued by the student, however, as she may attempt to transfer what Bakker and Bakker-Rabdau term an "overall guardianship" of her paper to the tutor. In other words, the client may hand over a great deal of her psychological space to the tutor—so much so that she now feels that the tutor can make decisions for her. The tutor, in effect, becomes her parent-figure, the guardian of the action space comprised by the paper. The student, moreover, may "welcome" such a takeover, and even "enjoy a sense of relief, knowing that [she] can take a vacation while [her] affairs are in good hands" (Bakker and Bakker-Rabdau 180).

This, of course, is a risk our writing center assumes through its positioning of its services as "expert" and "professional," provided by the oldest, most experienced and best qualified students on campus. Students seduced by these claims may become overly dependent on the tutor to provide assistance and await that tutor's verdict on what and how to write. Faced with these expectations, the tutor must be unwilling to pronounce a verdict on her client's draft and instead deploy the territorial weapon of definition to better clarify the psychological space of the tutorial. She reminds the student of what she can, and cannot, be reasonably expected to accomplish during the course of the tutorial. This is accomplished through rhetorical moves such as declaration ("I am not here to write your paper for you") and interrogation ("Can you explain how this sentence fits into this paragraph?"). Often the tutor will ask the student to write instead of making notes on that student's draft. This request defers the responsibility for writing to the student. And from the outset of the tutorial, tutors will request to see the student's assignment; this move defines the subsequent work of the tutorial in terms of the professor's territory, not the graduate tutor's territory. By reviewing the assignment with the tutee, the graduate tutor defers to an authority greater than her own, the authority of the instructor. Augmented by the weapon of self-definition, discussed above, this deferral positions the graduate tutor in the middle of what can be construed as a vertical continuum of authority, with the professor above and the tutee just below her.

Behavior Two: Warning

The behavior of "warning" entails making displays in order to "let intruders know they are trespassing" (Garner 30). An "intruder" in the writing center might be a student who wishes to drop a paper off with the staff and pick up edited copy later. Tutors address this contingency with the weapon of definition ("Please make an appointment; we would like to discuss your work in person"). On occasion, those intruders are faculty who, although well-intentioned, actually transgress the boundaries of the tutorial by attempting to dictate and thereby control, the specific terms by which their students will be served. One such faculty member insisted that the writing center staff serve, in effect, as his own proxy. He mandated that all of his students write exactly the same thesis statement, and he asked the tutors to make sure that his command was executed. This move, of course, greatly troubled the tutors who felt as if the action space of student texts and the psychological space of the tutorial itself would be greatly compromised. The tutors asked me to confront the faculty member on their behalf—which worked, at least temporarily, until the beginning of the next semester, when the faculty member in question returned to the writing center with new students in tow.

"Repeat after me," he said to them; "I am stupid and I can't write. That's why I'm in the writing center." The (tenured) faculty member then turned to the slack-jawed staff on duty, saying, "You know how I like these papers written," and left the room. The tutors deployed the weapon of definition as they told the now greatly troubled students, "It's OK. He's gone now. We're here to help you." This exchange has become a sad but productive tradition in our writing center—an opportunity for us at staff meetings to debrief and revisit some of our fundamental means of self-definition: we are kind, patient, supportive, and damn good at teaching writing. I trust the tutors to care for their damaged clients, and they trust me to intervene on their behalf with the faculty member should this be necessary. The exchange has also become a powerful means for graduate tutors to understand faculty psychology. The offending faculty member believes that he is in fact doing his students a favor by walking them down to the writing center. He believes he is placing their intellectual plight in perspective by casting grave aspersions on their abilities as writers. He believes he is being respectful of our authority by reminding us that we know what he prefers in student texts. Yet he does not understand his self-presentation: we define ourselves as a writing center—at UTT, and I would argue in the IWCA as a whole—against all those who would teach as he does.

Another prominent group of "intruders" is comprised of students who are required to visit the writing center as part of a writing assignment. This well-intentioned move on the part of faculty completely strips these students of any vestiges of intrinsic motivation, that innate drive to improve that is so vital to a strong, collaborative tutorial. "Required" students assume very little agency in tutorials and tend to defer completely to tutors, as evidenced through nonverbal cues. Tutees will slump back in their chairs, cross their arms on their chests, even push the paper in question in front of the tutor, thereby transferring all action and psychological space to the tutor. Tutors' attempts to generate productive conversation are typically met with silence, or, at best, an exasperated "My instructor told me to come here."[5] Again the behavior of defense serves as a warning, as tutors recount for the reticent student the purpose of a tutorial. If this gesture is not sufficient to encourage adequate participation, the tutor provides the student with a carbon-copy record attesting to the student's presence in the writing center, and the session ends. The student then takes that record to her instructor, who is accordingly warned that the writing center is unwilling to work with unmotivated students. On occasion, that faculty member will question the director about the tutorial; at this point, the director again deploys the weapon of defense as he warns his colleague about the problems inherent to requiring writing center attendance.

Significantly, self-definition is also a key element of the warning behaviors employed by graduate tutors. This is nowhere more apparent than in our ongoing tutor training program in which tutors follow widely-received guidelines[6] for effective tutoring while developing their own unique styles. A quick-witted tutor built her practice on humor, a technique she deployed to defuse the tension inherent to so many tutorials. Another former tutor gained a rep-

---

[5] These observations again draw from Niiler's ongoing action research project, previously noted in note #4.

[6] Tutor training is based in part on training manuals by Leigh Ryan (*The Bedford Guide for Writing Tutors*, Bedford Books, 1998); Christina Murphy and Steve Sherwood (*The St. Martin's Sourcebook for Writing Tutors*, St. Martin's, 1995); and Neal Lerner and Paula Gillespie (*The Allyn & Bacon Guide to Peer Tutoring*, Pearson Longman, 1999).

utation for her directness: she stood fast as a brick wall, actively resisting any attempt on the part of the student to transfer ownership of a paper. Another tutor used active listening techniques and deliberate choices of posture (sitting still, hands folded, and direct eye contact) to position himself as a thoughtful, deliberate, fully attuned consultant. These and other personal tutoring styles are key elements in tutors' ongoing self-definition and professional development. While I can insist that tutors adhere to a given outline for any tutorial (a process of greeting, definition of a problem, the positing of possible solutions, guided practice, independent practice, and closure), I cannot mandate style. If I attempt to do so, I am warned away, as was the case when I asked one loquacious tutor to cut down on the amount of small talk she made. The tutor responded by indicating that such small talk was indeed necessary to prepare the client for tutoring and that the client would have been much less amenable to tutoring otherwise.

Behavior Three:　Defense

As we have seen, territorial behavior helps graduate tutors acquire space in which to grow professionally as well as discourage, or warn, those who would trespass on that space. A territorialist perspective is also useful when considering how graduate tutors understand themselves—in particular, how they defend their new and burgeoning roles within the academy. Jeff has a B.A. in History with a Criminal Justice minor; he's worked in UTT's writing center for two years. Jeff is quick to note that he probably will not continue for his PhD because he views academic work as largely theoretical and thereby divorced from practical experience.

> I feel like much of what I do as a graduate student and an academic is a waste of time. I'm not contributing to anything, except to a circle of like-minded people. (Dillman)

While located within an academic setting, the writing center nonetheless represents, for Jeff, an alternative to this conception of academic life. The writing center is for him a place where theory meets practice, where he can "actually make a difference in students' lives by helping them reach their goals at the university" (Dillman). For Jeff, the writing center is a site of conversation and ultimately knowledge-making, as per Bruffee, who describes the same phenomenon in "Peer Tutoring and the 'Conversation of Mankind.'" Jeff notes that his classroom experience can be meaningfully employed in the tutorial through which he sees his role not so much as an academic within a discourse community closed off from the rest of the world but, instead, as an academic who "helps and serves" others. "Working in the writing center," Jeff says, "helps me *defend to myself* my decision to be an academic, at least for the time being. I would not be an academic otherwise" (Dillman; emphasis mine).

Graduate tutors are also quick to defend any perceived threat to the psychological space of the writing center through deploying weapons of definition and seduction. The former weapon is most commonly manifest through extensive paperwork. After each tutorial, the tutor completes a "Tutoring Record," which indicates in outline form the various topics discussed during the session. The "Record" effectively defines a given student as belonging to a given tutor; the student becomes an extension of that tutor's influence or psychological space. The tutor's choice of consulting strategy is subsequently defended in the "Personal Tutoring Report." The "Report," completed for each tutorial, expands upon the "Record" by prompting tutors to more fully develop the issues encountered in the session, as well as the tutoring strategies employed. Tutors are also asked to evaluate the effectiveness of the tutorial and consider how that tutorial might be improved. Further, tutors complete self-evaluation forms at the beginning, in the middle, and at the end of the academic year. I respond both orally and in writing to these evaluations with the idea that such conversation contributes to a tutor's developing sense of him or herself as a writing center professional.

This collection of documents serves to define a tutor's style and methods, especially with regard to the defense of psychological space. By carefully documenting each tutorial and demonstrating an ongoing commitment to professional development, graduate tutors defend their right to work in the writing center, thereby augmenting their professional status. In fact, many of these documents are used for staff development during regular staff meetings. Referring to their "Tutoring Records" and "Personal Tutoring Reports" in addition to outside readings, tutors debrief the rest of the staff on problematic or otherwise significant tutorials. Other tutors and the director then lend their commentary, questions, and constructive criticism to the conversation. The overarching goal is reflective practice, that is, a careful consideration of performance within the context of ongoing improvement. This emphasis on documentation further serves to defend tutors—and the writing center itself—against faculty and student misconceptions about the mission of the writing center. Faculty and students who are new to the writing center frequently complain that their papers are not perfect, even after a consultation. Yet these methods of documentation are usually enough to satisfy both student and faculty member as to the true objective of the tutorial: improvement, assistance, consultation, conversation, and not editing. Additionally, I use these and other related documents to create annual reports, the means by which, to some degree, the further existence of the writing center can be justified. Graduate tutors, therefore, participate directly in the ongoing defense of the institutional space comprised by the writing center.

Graduate tutors further defend their territory by deploying the weapon of seduction, that is, "the creation of an expectation of some greater good"

(Bakker and Bakker-Rabdau 190). Tutors "seduce" me into allowing them to retain their territory, not simply by doing a good job on a regular basis but also by finding new territories to acquire and thereby defend further. For example, two tutors proved to be extraordinarily proficient not only in tutorials but also as administrative assistants. These tutors claimed action space of their own in the writing center: Karen inventoried and ordered supplies, created schedule books, and drafted a series of documents that aided in the ongoing administration of the writing center. She sat at the receptionist's desk, in a receptionist's blue chair, a physical setting that allowed her ready access to timesheets, schedules, phone, and e-mail. Kathleen, in turn, painted and wallpapered the center. Both Karen and Kathleen did more than tutor—they helped acquire and subsequently defend their psychological space within the writing center, so much so that it is virtually impossible to enter the facility without feeling their indelible influence.

Behavior Four: Marking

This ongoing assumption of specific operational processes enables tutors to mark, through seduction, their action space in the writing center—that is, to indicate their ownership of it (Garner 30) by "creating the expectation of some greater good" (Bakker and Bakker-Rabdau 190). Tutors in this respect see their action space as multifaceted, requiring a rich variety of instructional, interpersonal, and administrative skills to maintain. The more territory that tutors mark in this regard, the more difficult it becomes to conceive of the position of tutoring in the writing center as limited to tutoring only. Tutors, in effect, become para-professionals, assuming a quasi-faculty status; in fact, in a kind of institutional affirmation of their profile, the university grants them faculty/staff parking privileges (but not faculty/staff salaries and benefits packages).

Secure within positions that permit and encourage a great deal of action and psychological space, tutors are quick to resist any administrative moves that would compromise those spaces. In one staff meeting, tutors voiced their concerns over a new performance evaluation rubric which would have required me to observe and then rate their tutoring on a Lickert scale. Such a move, they felt, would have forced them to surrender some of their action and psychological space. Some background is necessary here: at present, I do not spend a great deal of time in the writing center, preferring instead to allocate action and psychological territory to tutors while providing support for this work through brief daily exchanges, regular staff meetings, periodic individual conferences, reviews of tutors' written records, and regular debriefing with faculty and administration. This kind of management style, I suggest, demonstrates my trust in tutors' ability, while concurrently underscoring my support of their work. It is a largely unobtrusive strategy that by definition turns over a great deal of writing center territory to graduate tutors.

Deploying the weapon of definition, the tutors indicated that the proposed face-to-face observations and quantitative rankings would have quickly compromised a familiar management style and their high status. That said, the tutors then worked collaboratively with me to discern and articulate an evaluative rubric that would leave their territory more or less intact. The outcome was a rubric that rested largely on my formal documentation of the qualitative, albeit informal, documentation measures already in place. Tutors emerged from the meeting having (re)marked their territory. In another instance, graduate tutors resisted my suggestion to limit tutorials to 45 minutes or less, arguing that many students need substantial time to become comfortable and settle into a tutorial. Noting those same students' largely favorable evaluations of tutor performance, I conceded this point to the tutors. On both occasions, I reflected that I have, in fact, turned over so much territory to his tutors that, upon occasion, I feel as if I am an intruder in their writing center.

Yet this is as it should be. From the outset, I wanted the writing center to be a space wherein students could receive assistance with their writing and staff could receive preparation for future careers. It was my goal to provide graduate students with an opportunity for professional development *within an academic discipline*. In fact, the writing center's mission is articulated in terms of real academic work: teaching, scholarship, and service ("Information for Faculty"). Before the writing center began, there was a lack of reallife, academically oriented opportunities for professional development for graduate students. The English Department offers a Masters degree, but candidates have no opportunity to parlay their academic skills in the workplace, at least on campus. In effect, I wanted to create junior colleagues, true teaching assistants in an emerging field. Territorially, I claimed the action space of the writing center on behalf of my graduate tutors. The graduate tutors, in turn, have claimed the territory of writing center administration and writing center tutorial, as largely their own.

Conclusion

Graduate tutors are engaged in a myriad of complex daily struggles to acquire, warn, defend, and mark territory, all for the sake of conducting the seemingly simple business of helping other students with writing assignments. They acquire writing center territory by defining their work in terms of their largely privileged status on our campus; their considerable authority and experience as writers creates an expertise-based model for tutoring rather than a more commonly articulated peer tutoring model. As part of the acquisition process, they self-define, employing careful rhetorical strategies that position them as consultants. Seeking to deliver on the beneficent promise of honing students' writing skills, they create the "expectation of a greater good": better writers. And with the understanding that this promise may in fact be seductive, they work to defer the work of improving a text to the student herself.

Once having acquired writing center territory, tutors are quick to deploy weapons of definition and self-definition to warn off potential faculty or student intruders: those who would attempt to bend the course of a tutorial to their own ends or those who enter the center merely to claim an artifact (an affidavit of attendance) as opposed to a consultation. These same weapons, augmented by seduction, again come into play as tutors defend their personal tutoring styles to me and, in fact, attempt to locate new action and psychological space to acquire and defend. Tutors, finally, firmly and indelibly mark the positions they have so far acquired, warned intruders away from, and defended by deploying weapons of definition and seduction. With a rich litany of tutoring and administrative experience under their belts and at their fingertips, tutors—like many faculty—are loathe to surrender or, at the very least, compromise the significant action and psychological space they currently maintain.

These tutors' positions are not made any easier through the writing center's unique institutional juncture: it is not quite a classroom, not quite an office. It is staffed by individuals who are not quite students, but not quite faculty either. As its director, I am often physically absent yet nonetheless psychologically present. Yet to the extent that graduate tutors are able to begin to claim that space as their own, the writing center proves to be a fertile ground for professional development, a site wherein tutors claim significant power through the territory they occupy. (It is not at all coincidental, then, that the weapons of definition and self-definition are cited in each of the four behaviors covered by this chapter.) That power, moreover, is the power of professional identity, the sense that through the daily struggle of writing center work, tutors are beginning to articulate who they are, what they believe, and why those things matter.

Among current tutors, there is a sure sense of professional growth, a growth augmented by weapons of self-definition. Consider the terms Sara uses to describe her personal style: she is "committed to the cause of tutoring, rational in approaching all situations, and courteous under all but the worst situations" (Steinbrueck). Note, too, how Jim defines himself:

> I am trained in and skilled at my work, and I seek ongoing education to improve my tutoring skills. I am aware of the need to be more than a reader/writer/editor. I must also be an educator, a motivator, and seek to add to my clients' skills while reaffirming the skills they already possess. (D'Avignon)

Territoriality, finally, becomes not only a theoretical means of considering the value of the work of graduate students in the writing center, but also a hugely practical method of understanding how to effectively mentor graduate students in the writing center. The director, or any writing center administrator, must accept the fact that graduate tutors, like student tutees, will learn through myriad ways and means—that no one form of supervision is in fact appropriate. As Kathleen, a former tutor, puts it, "To be a professional, I need to be free: free to learn, to innovate, and to improve myself and my work" (Dunsavage).

Writing center administrators must understand that the age, autonomy, academic and work experience of graduate students can help create a highly self-motivated staff. The director must therefore be able to envision a writing center humming along nicely in his or her absence. Such concessions of psychological and action space are not wholesale surrenders of the writing center: as I have noted, I am often needed to assist with the ongoing work of acquisition, warning, defense, and marking. Yet such concessions demonstrate trust: a trust that graduate tutors will parlay into sound professional practice.

Works Cited

Bakker, Cornelis, and Marianne K. Bakker-Rabdau. *No Trespassing! Explorations in Human Territoriality.* San Francisco: Chandler, 1973.

Bruffee, Kenneth A. "Peer Tutoring and the 'Conversation of Mankind.'" In *Landmark Essays on Writing Centers.* Ed. Christina Murphy and Joe Law. Davis, CA: Hermagoras, 1995. 87–98.

Carino, Peter. "Writing Centers and Writing Programs: Local and Communal Politics." In *The Politics of Writing Centers.* Ed. Jane Nelson and Kathy Evertz. Portsmouth, NH: Heinemann/Boynton/Cook, 2001. 1–14.

_____. "Reading Our Own Words: Rhetorical Analysis and the Institutional Discourse of Writing Centers." *Writing Center Research: Extending the Conversation.* Ed. Paula Gillespie, Alice Gillam, Lady Falls Brown, and Byron Stay. Mahwah, NJ: Lawrence Erlbaum Associates, 2002. 91–110.

_____. "Power and Authority in Peer Tutoring." *The Center Will Hold: Critical Perspectives on Writing Center Scholarship.* Ed. Michael A. Pemberton and Joyce Kinkead. Logan: Utah State UP, 2003. 96–113.

D'Avignon, Jim. Personal interview. 9 May 2003.

Dillman, Jeff. Personal interview. 1 February 2005.

Dunsavage, Kathleen. Personal interview. 12 May 2003.

Ede, Lisa. "Writing as a Social Process: A Theoretical Foundation for Writing Centers?" 1989. *Landmark Essays on Writing Centers.* Ed. Christina Murphy and Joe Law. Davis, CA: Hermagoras, 1995. 99–108.

Garner, Karen. "Territorial Tug-of-War: Ownership Disputes and Solutions in University Writing Centers." Unpublished Master's thesis. The University of Texas at Tyler, 2001.

Grimm, Nancy Maloney. *Good Intentions: Writing Center Work for Postmodern Times.* Portsmouth, NH: Heinemann/Boynton/Cook, 1999.

Jordan, Thomas. "The Uses of Territories in Conflicts: A Psychological Perspective." *Online Journal of Peace and Conflict Resolution* 1(2). 78 pars. May 1998. 15 June 2007 <http://www.trinstitute.org/ojpcr/1_2jordan.htm>.

Keith, Karen. Personal interview. 15 June 2003.

Lunsford, Andrea. "Collaboration, Control, and the Idea of a Writing Center." 1991. *Landmark Essays on Writing Centers.* Ed. Christina Murphy and Joe Law. Davis, CA: Hermagoras, 1995. 109–116.

Niiler, Lucas P. "Information for Faculty." The University of Texas at Tyler Writing Center Homepage. 25 September 2003. <http://www.uttyler.edu/writingcenter>.

_____. "Information for Students." The University of Texas at Tyler Writing Center Homepage. 25 September 2003. <http://www.uttyler.edu/writingcenter>.

North, Stephen M. "The Idea of a Writing Center." 1984. *Landmark Essays on Writing Centers*. Ed. Christina Murphy and Joe Law. Davis, CA: Hermagoras, 1995. 71–86.

_____. "Revisiting 'The Idea of a Writing Center.'" *The Writing Center Journal* 15.1 (1994): 7–19.

Palmeri, Jason. "Transgressive Hybridity: Reflections on the Authority of the Peer Writing Tutor." *Writing Lab Newsletter* 25.1 (2000): 9–11.

Sack, Robert David. *Human Territoriality: Its Theory and History*. Cambridge Studies in Historical Geography 7. Cambridge: Cambridge UP, 1987.

Steinbrueck, Sara. Personal interview. 10 June 2003.

Biographies

Julie A. Eckerle is Assistant Professor of English at the University of Minnesota, Morris. In addition to her work on (and in) writing centers, she has published articles on early modern romance and early modern women's writing and recently co-edited *Genre and Women's Life Writing in Early Modern England*.

Cinthia Gannett is an Associate Professor of Writing and Director of the Loyola Writing Center and Writing Across the Curriculum at Loyola College in Maryland. She was at the University of New Hampshire for many years before that and directed the WAC Program and the Connors Writing Center at various times. Her current research projects include the application of post-colonial translation studies to writing center work, Jesuit rhetorical pedagogy, and archival studies in composition.

Christopher LeCluyse directs the writing center at Westminster College, Salt Lake City, where he teaches writing in various disciplines, composition pedagogy, and history of the English language. He also writes language arts materials for Holt, Rinehart, and Winston and sings professionally with Conspirare and other ensembles.

Michael Mattison is the Director of the Writing Center and Assistant Professor of English at Boise State University. When not working with writers or consultants, he spends a good deal of time at the local post office, trying to convince the administration to invest in a time machine so that letters such as his can be delivered.

Sue Mendelsohn is the Saint Louis University Writing Center coordinator and a former graduate assistant at the University of Texas at Austin Undergraduate Writing Center. Sue is a co-founder of *Praxis: A Writing Center Journal*.

Melissa Nicolas is Writing Program Director and Assistant Professor of English at Rochester Institute of Technology. Her publications include *By Any Other Name: Writing Groups Inside and Outside the Classroom* (co-edited with Beverly Moss and Nels Highberg) as well as articles in *Lore, Academic Exchange Quarterly, Writing Lab Newsletter, MP: An International Feminist Journal, Praxis*, and chapters in several edited collections. She is currently conducting a qualitative study on the effects of hurricanes Katrina and Rita on students in first-year writing classes.

Luke Niiler is director of the Writing Center and Associate Professor of English at the University of Alabama. His research interests include quantitative analyses of writing center practice. He has a B.A. in English from Gettysburg College, and an M.A. and Ph.D. in English from the State University of New York at Buffalo.

Brooke Rollins is an Assistant Professor of English at Louisiana State University, where she teaches courses in rhetorical theory and history and composition studies.

She has recently published articles in *College English, Rhetoric Society Quarterly,* and *The Velvet Light Trap.*

Karen Rowan is Assistant Professor of English and Writing Center Director at Morgan State University. In addition to writing about graduate student administrators and administrative professional development, she is currently co-editing a collection of new essays on the intersections of race, racism, and literacy in writing center practice and discourse.

Leigh Ryan directs the University of Maryland Writing Center. In addition to articles on writing center theory and practice, she is the author of *The Bedford Guide for Writing Tutors* (4th edition with Lisa Zimmerelli). A former officer in the International Writing Centers Association and the Mid-Atlantic Writing Centers Association, she currently serves on their executive boards.

Nathalie Singh-Corcoran is an Assistant Professor of English and Writing Center Coordinator at West Virginia University. She teaches courses in writing center praxis, composition, and English education and is co-director of the National Writing Project at WVU. She has served on the International Writing Centers Association board and as chair of the IWCA Research Awards Committee and has co-authored a chapter in an award winning writing center book.

Trixie G. Smith is Director of the Writing Center at Michigan State University where she teaches courses in writing center theory and practice and works with the Tier II Writing Program (WID). Before arriving at MSU, she worked at Middle Tennessee State University in various positions, including Writing Center Director, TA Coordinator, and Writing Minor advisor. Her publications include *COMPbiblio: Leaders and Influences in Composition Theory and Practice* (co-edited with Allison D. Smith and Karen Wright) and articles in *Research Strategies* and *Southern Discourse.*

Helen Snively holds an Ed.D. from the Harvard Graduate School of Education, where she studied cultural differences that affect writing and the psychological basis of writing blocks. Since 1981, as the Thesis Therapist, she has supported doctoral students and new academics in both completing their programs and becoming better writers.

Katherine E. Tirabassi is an Assistant Professor of English at Keene State College in New Hampshire. Previously, she served as Graduate Assistant Director of the University of New Hampshire's Robert J. Connors Writing Center. Her research interests include writing center theory and practice, writing across the curriculum and histories of writing instruction.

Shevaun E. Watson is an Assistant Professor of English at the University of South Carolina. She has served on the Executive Boards of IWCA and SWCA. Her research interests include writing centers, the history of rhetoric, early America, and women's literacy. Her current book project examines early African American rhetorics.

Evelyn Westbrook collaborated with peers Trixie Smith and Brooke Rollins on this chapter while completing her M.A. in English at the University of South Carolina. Evelyn worked as a writing center consultant at USC and also at the University of Texas at Austin, where she completed her doctoral coursework.

Amy Zenger, an Assistant Professor of English at the American University of Beirut, directs the Writing Center and teaches composition. She is the author, with Bronwyn Williams, of *Popular Culture and Representations of Literacy,* which studies images of reading and writing in Hollywood movies.

Lisa Zimmerelli is Assistant Professor of English and Director of the online Effective Writing Center at the University of Maryland University College. Lisa has presented at conferences on writing center theory and pedagogy, and co-authored the fourth edition of *The Bedford Guide for Writing Tutors* with Leigh Ryan.

Index